Did Pope Pius XII Help the Jews?

Vobis, dilectissimi filii, qui in infestum tenis casus expeditionibus renuntiis vel ac sedulam admirabium operam ultris navalis ad Jesu Christi Regnum asseugnam promisodum, paramenta in Domino benedicimus, animo exoptantes "ut clarispetem anima, D. N. J. Christi in vobis et vos in illo" (2 Thess. 1. 12).

3 - X - 39

Pius PP. XII

Did Pope Pius XII Help the Jews?

Margherita Marchione

PAULIST PRESS
New York • Mahwah, NJ

This book is affectionately dedicated to His Holiness Pope Benedict XVI

The author graciously acknowledges the financial assistance given by the Filangieri Foundation to honor the eighteenth-century Italian jurist Gaetano Filangieri, who has influenced the study of jurisprudence. She is grateful to its founder, Lawrence Auriana, president of Federated Investment Corporation, for this contribution.

Unless otherwise noted, the scripture quotations outlined herein are from the New Revised Standard Version Bible, copyright © 1989 by the Division of Christian Education of the National Council of Churches of Christ in the U.S.A. Used by permission.

Cover design by Lynn Else
Book design by John Eagleson

Library of Congress Cataloging-in-Publication Data

Marchione, Margherita.
    Did Pope Pius XII help the Jews? / Margherita Marchione.
        p. cm.
    Includes bibliographical references and index.
    ISBN-13: 978-0-8091-4476-1 (alk. paper)
    1. Pius XII, Pope, 1876-1958 – Relations with Jews. 2. Catholic Church – Relations – Judaism. 3. Judaism – Relations – Catholic Church. 4. World War, 1939-1945 – Religious aspects – Catholic Church. 5. Holocaust, Jewish (1939-1945) I. Title.
    BX1378.M264 2007
    282.092 – dc22

                                                                    2007012562

Published by Paulist Press
997 Macarthur Boulevard
Mahwah, New Jersey 07430

www.paulistpress.com

Printed and bound in the
United States of America

Contents

Foreword

One of the distinct blessings of the thirteen years that I spent in Rome, both as a student and as an official of the Roman Curia, was coming to know more directly the extraordinary care of the Servant of God, Pope Pius XII, for the Jewish people during the time of their persecution by Adolf Hitler and his National Socialist government. The true story of Pope Pius XII's anguish over the evils of National Socialism and his actions to save those destined for extermination in the concentration camps was not difficult to hear and witness in the Eternal City.

As a seminarian in the late 1960s, I was blessed to hear Rabbi Joseph Lichten speak about the delicacy of the situation in which Pope Pius XII found himself in caring for his Jewish brothers and sisters, and the Pope's prudent and yet strong action to save the lives of so many Jews. Rabbi Lichten, a devoutly religious man and outstanding scholar, who knew well the situation of Pope Pius XII's response to the deplorable plight of the Jewish people, did not hesitate to offer grateful praise for the Pope's extraordinary care for his people.

During my years of study at the Pontifical Gregorian University, both as a seminarian and as a priest, I heard directly from the Jesuit Fathers how their confrères at the university during the German occupation of Rome housed securely a good number of Jewish people, including the chief rabbi of Rome. They told how, when the Gestapo officers arrived to inspect the university's buildings in search of hidden Jews, the porter would delay them so that the Jesuit Fathers and Brothers could hide their treasured guests.

I recall seeing the marble plaque placed in the Augustinianum Patristic Institute by the Jewish people in order to pay tribute to the Augustinian Friars who had given safe shelter to a number of Jews who were in danger of either direct execution or deportation to the death camps. It was common knowledge that other houses of religious and institutions of the Holy See had done everything possible to save our Jewish brothers and sisters from the genocide intended by Hitler.

In all of the reports that I heard and in all of the visual evidence of the care of Jewish people by institutions of the Church, there was never any question that all of the activity on behalf of the Jewish people was carried out not only with the blessing of Pope Pius XII but also at his urging and explicit direction. Recently, I have read about the journal of the cloistered Augustinian nuns at the Basilica of the Santi Quattro Coronati in Rome, from the time of the German occupation, which records explicitly Pope Pius XII's order that monasteries and convents, even cloistered communities, receive the Jewish people as guests and hide them from their persecutors.

Pope Pius XII, called the Angelic Pastor (*Pastor Angelicus*) by the faithful who experienced his most compassionate and heroic care during the terrible years of World War II, unfailingly held the Jewish people in his shepherd's heart. In the most delicate and dangerous situation for the Jews, he acted as a true shepherd of souls, not as politician or secular leader. He, personally and with the cooperation of so many faithful, especially the religious communities, saved as many lives as was humanly possible. At the same time, he strove to avoid any action that, while it may have won for him some notoriety, would only have increased the fury of the Nazi persecution of the Jews.

The few accounts of what I directly learned about Pope Pius XII's care of the Jewish people during the deplorable Nazi persecution is a small part of the story that has been told and is told, with honesty and in its integrity, by Sister Margherita Marchione of the Religious Teachers Filippini. Sister Margherita had the privilege of meeting Pope Pius XII, an encounter that left her with a strong and lasting impression of his holiness. It is the heroic holiness of the life of Pope Pius XII, of which Sister Margherita caught a glimpse in her personal encounter, that has inspired her to devote her considerable gifts of mind and heart to the work of presenting to the world the truth about the important chapter in the life of the Pope concerning his devoted love of and care for the Jewish people.

Sister Margherita has already written six books about Pope Pius XII. Most recently, she has written *Crusade of Charity*, based on her thorough research of the published documents of the Holy See's Secret Archives pertaining to the Second World War. *Crusade of Charity* tells the story of the Holy See's formidable efforts, inspired and directed by Pope Pius XII, to help families of every faith find their members who were missing because of the war.

Sister Margherita's research and writing is important in itself, for it tells a story of heroic charity, which our world needs to hear. It is made even more important by the spreading of defamatory accusations against Pope Pius XII over the past four decades, especially regarding his relationship to the Jewish people. For whatever reasons and motives, a number of authors, Catholics and Jews, have claimed that Pope Pius XII was anti-Semitic and, therefore, sympathetic to the position of Hitler and National Socialism. Their writings, which are often written in a popular style and have received extensive and favorable comment from the media, have led many to believe uncritically their claims. Thank God, therefore, for the writings of Sister Margherita, together with those of several other distinguished Catholic and Jewish scholars, which make evident the truth of the matter.

In her continued work to present the truth about Pope Pius XII's unfailing and, indeed, heroic charity in addressing the plight of the persecuted Jews, Sister Margherita now addresses directly and succinctly the question of whether Pope Pius XII helped the Jews during World War II. She asks the question, in particular, in view of the text that appears under the image of Pope Pius XII in the Memorial to the Holocaust in Yad Vashem and that is heavily influenced by the just-mentioned defamatory and false claims. In responding to the question, she respectfully requests that the Memorial to the Holocaust correct the text that it now displays and bestow upon Pope Pius XII the title "Righteous Among the Nations."

Bringing together, in a succinct form, the fruit of her extensive research, Sister Margherita provides the proofs for a resoundingly affirmative response to the question which has inspired this, her most recent work. Her response reflects her always deep respect for the Jewish people and her profound sorrow over the demonic persecution that they, along with others, suffered at the hands of Adolf Hitler and his agents. At the same time, her response reflects her well-founded conviction that telling the truth about Pope Pius XII will best honor the Jewish victims of National Socialism and will most help us to prevent the repetition of such unspeakable crimes against God and humanity in the future.

I am honored to write the foreword to Sister Margherita's latest work. In presenting her work, I pray that it will be read widely and that it will achieve its stated end, the long-overdue recognition of Pope Pius XII as "Righteous Among the Nations" by the Memorial to the Holocaust in Yad Vashem. As we approach the fiftieth anniversary of the death of Pope Pius XII, let us hope that the desire which Sister Margherita Marchione expressed in her first book about Pope Pius XII may be fulfilled: "Time is the unfolding of truth. One reads in Ecclesiasticus (3:1–8) that 'there is an appointed time for everything, and a time for every affair.' After fifty years of misrepresentation of Pope Pius XII's role during the Holocaust, it is now time to tell the true story and acknowledge his leadership" (*Yours Is a Precious Witness: Memoirs of Jews and Catholics in Wartime Italy,* Paulist Press, 1997, p. 181).

Sister Margherita entitled her autobiography *The Fighting Nun: My Story.* Sister, indeed, is a fighter for the truth and for love, in the Scriptural sense of the term. She has fought "the good fight" (1 Tim. 6:12) on behalf of the truth about the Servant of God Pope Pius XII. We are all in her debt. May Almighty God reward her.

> *The Most Reverend Raymond Leo Burke*
> *Archbishop of Saint Louis*
> *Feast of the Chair of Saint Peter, Apostle*
> *February 22, 2007*

Overview
Did Pius XII Help Jews?

It is historically correct to say that during World War II Pope Pius XII, through his bishops, nuncios, and local priests, mobilized Catholics to assist Jews, Allied soldiers, and prisoners of war. There is a considerable body of scholarly opinion that is convinced Pius XII is responsible for having saved five hundred thousand to eight hundred thousand Jewish lives. In addition, one cannot ignore the views of those Jewish scholars who have defended and praised Pius XII. They include, among others, Pinchas Lapide, Jenö Levai, and Dr. Joseph Lichten, as well as historian Michael Tagliacozzo, Sir Martin Gilbert, and Rabbi David Dalin, whose current scholarly contributions in defense of the Pope must be added to the work of past writers.

In his book *Adolf Hitler,* John Toland wrote: "The Church, under the Pope's guidance, had (by June 1943) already saved the lives of more Jews than all other churches, religious institutions and rescue organizations combined, and was presently hiding thousands of Jews in monasteries, convents and Vatican City itself.... The British and Americans, despite lofty pronouncements, had not only avoided taking any meaningful action but gave sanctuary to few persecuted Jews"(Doubleday, 1976, 2:865).

During World War II, the Pope provided false identification papers to potential victims of the Nazis and the Fascists. He ordered Vatican buildings, churches, convents, and monasteries to open their doors and find hiding places for Jews and other refugees. The following statement by German leaders is revealing: "The Pope has repudiated the National Socialist New European Order ... and makes himself the mouthpiece of the Jewish war criminals."

Israeli foreign minister Golda Meir stated: "We share in the grief of humanity.... When fearful martyrdom came to our people in the decade of Nazi terror, the voice of the Pope was raised for the victims.... We mourn a great servant of peace."

Nor can Albert Einstein's statement be ignored: "Only the Church stood squarely across the path of Hitler's campaign for suppressing the truth.... The Church alone has had the courage and persistence to stand for intellectual truth and moral freedom. I am forced thus to confess that what I once despised, I now praise unreservedly" (*Time* magazine, December 23, 1940).

History records Pope Pius XII's efforts to avoid World War II. His words were prophetic: "Nothing is lost by peace. Everything may be lost by war" (August 24, 1939). According to the *New York Times,* months before the war, Pope Pius XII invited the prime ministers and foreign ministers of five European countries (Germany, Great Britain, France, Italy, and Poland) to confer in Vatican City. He suggested that the meeting be held as soon as possible. He would open the first session in person and would put his palace and staff at the disposal of the plenipotentiaries. He would take no part personally but, if needed, he would be at the disposal of the conference through his secretary of state as counselor and conciliator. He further suggested that the aim of the conference would be to settle amicably the German-Polish dispute and eventually to begin the settlement of other problems.

The *New York Times* article, by Jules Sauerwein, concluded: "Until now the Pope's proposal has been kept closely secret. That he has made it, is a mark of his high intelligence and exceptional courage. He believes it his duty to make this proposal so as to save Europe from war, even though he is not sure he will succeed." The editorial evaluated the political situation: "As Cardinal Pacelli, Pope Pius XII showed himself to be so devoted a friend of peace and so tireless an emissary of better understanding that it is wholly natural that he should now seek to use the authority of his great office to avert the threat of war in Europe."

Honest students of history must look skeptically at those accounts of Pope Pius XII's life which ignore relevant facts or rely on dubious or tainted sources (such as Soviet and Nazi propaganda) to make their case. Rather one can find persuasive evidence — in the form of news reports, testimony at the Nuremberg trials, documents in foreign archives, and research of reputable Jewish, Catholic, and other historians — that the Catholic Church consistently assisted Jewish victims of Nazi anti-Semitism. This fact is attested perhaps most strongly by the countless Jewish religious leaders, scholars, statesmen, journalists, and other dignitaries who have praised Pope Pius XII for his courage, compassion, and leadership.

The Holy See's position regarding the attempt to exterminate the Jewish people, with the consequent murder of millions of Jews, is that the *Shoah* was an immense tragedy. This was affirmed by Pope John Paul II at the Yad Vashem Monument on March 23, 2000, and confirmed by His Holiness, Benedict XVI, at the Auschwitz extermination camp on May 28, 2006. The memory of those terrible events must be a warning to eliminate conflicts and respect the legitimate rights of all peoples.

Yad Vashem is the national Holocaust memorial of the Jewish people in Israel, established by the Israeli Parliament in 1953. It consists of museums and monuments as well as research, teaching, and resource centers. Yad Vashem, which means a mountain and a name, is taken from the biblical verse Isaiah 56:5: "I will give, in my house and within my walls, a monument . . . that shall not be cut off."

Pius XII deserves to be recognized by Yad Vashem for having saved the lives of persecuted Jews. According to Jewish historian Michael Tagliacozzo, documents clearly prove that, in the early hours of the morning of October 16, 1943, Pius XII was informed of the round-up of the Jews in Rome. He immediately had German ambassador Ernst von Weizsäcker called and ordered secretary of state Luigi Maglione to energetically protest the Jews' arrest, asking that similar actions be stopped. If this did not happen, the Pope would denounce it publicly. In addition, by his initiative he had a letter of protest sent through Bishop Alois Hudal to the military commander in Rome, General Rainer Stahel, requesting that the persecution of Jews cease immediately. As a result of these protests, the operation providing for two days of arrests and deportations was interrupted at 2:00 p.m. the same day. Pius XII's protest was published in the Vatican's official publication of World War II documents.

2

Yad Vashem

Does Pius XII Deserve This Honor?

As far back as the days of the Romans, Jews had established themselves in Italy. Indeed, Jews contributed to the struggle for freedom in the nineteenth century; they were educated and had obtained prominent positions in all fields; Italian Jews retained their deep respect for ethical concepts, their culture, their heritage.

The World War II record of the Jews and the Catholic Church in Italy shows that Pope Pius XII, through his network of apostolic delegates throughout the world, was able to save the lives of thousands of Jews, including those who did not convert to Catholicism, during the Holocaust. Yad Vashem honors non-Jews who helped save Jews during the Shoah.

Early on, Italian foreign minister Giuseppe Saragat came to the defense of Pius XII: "I am convinced Pius XII was a great Pope and that the campaign against him is orchestrated for partisans. So many years after his death, this is unacceptable not just for Catholics, but for all men of good will. . . . Innumerable episodes reveal the spirit behind Pius XII's activity, especially here in Rome ...where there is living testimony from all citizens on Pius XII's work; moreover, instead of going to a safe place protected by Allied troops...he stayed in his place, in the middle of the storm, giving aid to neighborhoods stricken by the fury of the war, and trying to pry innocent victims away from Nazi barbarism....In any event, the controversy that has broken out over the memory of Pius XII is not a cultural debate; it is founded on calumnies and lies that have nothing to do with historical and cultural research. In the debates against Pius XII we see the cold, calculating propaganda of those trying to excuse Nazism from horrific crimes by making the Roman Catholic Church co-responsible."

As we approach the fiftieth anniversary of the death of Pope Pius XII on October 9, 1958, we ask Yad Vashem to posthumously recognize and honor him as "Righteous Among the Nations." Since 1962, many non-Jews who saved Jewish lives during the Holocaust have been honored by the Jewish community in Israel. Among those who received the title of "Righteous Among the Nations" are Monsignor Angelo Rotta and Cardinal Pietro Palazzini. The consensus among Catholics is that no one deserves this honor more than Pope Pius XII. Not only would this gesture be much appreciated worldwide, but it would then be possible to eliminate the false phraseology under his photo that is disturbing to many Catholics.

Comments follow the four erroneous statements displayed beneath the Yad Vashem photo of Pope Pius XII:

1. *"Pius XII's reaction toward the killing of Jews during the period of the Holocaust is controversial. In 1933, as the Vatican secretary of state, in order to maintain the rights of the Church in Germany, he signed a concordat with the Nazi regime even at the price of recognizing the racist Nazi regime. When he was elected Pope in 1939, he put aside an encyclical against racism and anti-Semitism prepared by his predecessor."*

This statement is false. Not only is the first part unfair and misleading, but the second is demonstrably untrue. The 1933 concordat was not, as the caption implies, a friendly agreement with Nazi Germany, much less an endorsement of its wicked ideology; rather, it was a defense mechanism necessary to protect the prerogatives of the Church against a ruthless totalitarian state. It was and remains a perfectly legitimate moral act, not a capitulation to evil. The concordat — which is frequently cited but almost never read — does not imply any kind of philosophical agreement with Hitler's regime. In fact, the supplemental protocol to article 32 states that the concordat "does not involve any sort of limitation of official and prescribed preaching and interpretation of the dogmatic and moral principles of the Church." That the Catholic Church utilized this freedom to oppose Hitler is proven by the Nazi regime's subsequent brutalities against the Catholic Church — the closing of Catholic institutions and the arrest, imprisonment, and execution of religious, as well as prominent Catholic laymen. Had the concordat "silenced" the Church, as is now sometimes claimed, this conflict would not have happened.

Pius XI died before he could read the pages of the draft encyclical against racism and anti-Semitism. Nor did his successor, Pius XII, read them. Instead, he wrote his own encyclical, *Summi Pontificatus,* which dealt with racism and totalitarianism. In it, Pius XII made abundantly clear his judgment of the German aggression. At the start of World War II, because the encyclical was so anti-Hitler, the Royal Air Force dropped eighty-eight thousand copies of it over Germany.

2. *"Although reports about the assassination of Jews reached the Vatican, the Pope did not protest either by speaking out or in writing."*

This is not true. Whenever Pius XII spoke out, there was immediate retaliation by the Nazis. There were more than sixty protests! The so-called "silence" of Pope Pius XII is a myth. Eugenio Pacelli was not "silent." As papal nuncio to Germany (1917–29), then Vatican secretary of state (1930–39) and Pope Pius XII (1939–58), he spoke out against the evils of his age: racism, ethnic and religious hatreds, nationalism, militarism, war crimes, and atrocities against noncombatants. His statements

were a continuation of those issued by his predeces-
sors, Benedict XV and Pope Pius XI. His first encyclical,
Summi Pontificatus, issued just weeks after the start
of World War II, emphasized the unity of the human
race, as expressed in Catholic theology. It is a direct
condemnation of the anti-Semitic racism of the Nazis
and remained the pontiff's position throughout the war.
Moreover, *L'Osservatore Romano* (the Vatican newspaper) and Vatican Radio were authorized, sustained, and
often scripted by Pius XII.

In 1939, immediately after the Nazi invasion of Poland,
the Vatican defended Jews by name. Vatican Radio condemned Nazi atrocities in Poland, revealing the horrors
of Hitler's war machine to the entire world. In January
1940, Vatican Radio explicitly declared: "Jews and Poles
are being herded into separate ghettos, hermetically sealed
and pitifully inadequate for the economic subsistence of
the millions destined to live there....It adds up to a
fearful total and a tremendous responsibility: one more
grievous affront to the moral conscience of mankind; one
more contemptuous insult to the law of nations; one more
open thrust at the heart of the Christian Father [Pope
Pius XII], who grieves with his dear Poland, and begs for
peace with decency and justice from the throne of grace."

3. *"In December of 1942, he did not participate in the*
   condemnation by members of the Allies regarding
   the killing of Jews. Even when the Jews were being

> *deported from Rome to Auschwitz, the Pope did not intervene."*

After that first day, the SS were ordered to stop the deportation of the Jews in Rome. According to Jewish historian Michael Tagliacozzo, a survivor who took refuge in the Vatican, Pius XII did indeed intervene. On October 26, 2000, Zenit News Agency interviewed Tagliacozzo, who praised Pope Pius XII's wartime conduct and refuted those who accused him and the Holy See of not doing enough to save Jews persecuted by the Nazis.

Harold Tittmann Jr. was President Franklin Delano Roosevelt's chief diplomat in Rome during the Nazi occupation of Rome. His book *Inside the Vatican of Pius XII: The Memoir of an American Diplomat during World War II,* published in 2004, is an excellent and balanced discussion of Pius XII's wartime statements, and praises the Pope for his intelligent use of anti-Nazi language. In fact, on pp. 122–24 Tittmann concludes: "The Holy Father chose the better path...and thereby saved many lives."

4. *"He maintained a neutral position except toward the end of the war when he appealed on behalf of the government of Hungary and of Slovakia. His silence and the absence of directives obliged the clergy in Europe to decide independently how they should behave toward the persecuted Jews."*

Both statements are erroneous. Pius XII's telegram of June 25, 1944, to Admiral Miklós Horthy, the regent in Budapest, was not the only personal protest message. The historical record shows that the clergy and members of the Church were ordered by Pope Pius XII to protect all refugees and Jews. Pope Pius XII was not "neutral" during the war. He judged everyone fairly. He condemned the Third Reich in his first encyclical, *Summi Pontificatus,* issued just weeks after the beginning of World War II.

In his 1939 Christmas address, Pius XII laid out five principles for peace, one of which was "that the real needs and the just demands of racial minorities" be respected. At that time, Jews were among the most endangered minorities. Pius XII's teaching on human rights was clear. Given the subsequent, ruthless extermination of Jews and other racial minorities by the Nazis, Pius XII's Christmas address must be seen as prophetic. At the same time, he created both the Pontifical Relief Commission and the Vatican Information Office in order to help feed, shelter, nurse, and protect anyone who was in need, regardless of race, nationality, or creed. Even though he was not an actual belligerent in the conflict, everyone knew that his sympathies were with the Allies and their cause. This is proven, not just by his warm correspondence with President Franklin Delano Roosevelt, but especially by his support for various German plots to overthrow Hitler.

◆ ◆ ◆

Upon my request regarding the criteria used at Yad Vashem, Dr. Mordecai Paldiel, director of the Department for "Righteous Among the Nations," responded on June 20, 2006: "The basic and underlying criteria is risk to one's life and personal safety when affording aid to Jews." He also added that he was interested in the directives received "from the hands of Pius XII to care for Jews." Perhaps the following information will enlighten the members of the public commission at Yad Vashem.

In 1984, a psychiatrist and a theologian — two Jews who survived the Holocaust — began an interesting dialogue on life and religious experiences. This dialogue between Victor E. Frankl and Pinchas Lapide, entitled *A Quest for God and the Meaning of Life,* has now been published in Italian. In their search for truth there is an intense interdisciplinary exchange on well-being and salvation, between psychotherapy and theology, science and faith. It is a precious dialog on suffering and compunction, but also on love and the meaning of life in order to comprehend the limits of one's own knowledge and to be open to true tolerance.

Forty years after the *Shoah,* one is surprised to read Frankl's reference to the help given to his brother and family by Pope Pius XII during the Holocaust (86–87). It is most revealing: "Before his deportation to Auschwitz where he and his wife died, for several years my brother and family were hidden from the Nazis and the

Fascists in Italy. During this period, until they were captured by the Nazis, they lived in a small town under
the protection of Pope Pius XII, who supplied all their
needs. I recently learned that this Pope entrusted them to
the care of his secretary, Giovanni Battista Montini, the
future Pope Paul VI. My brother represented the group of
Jews living in this town who had given him the honor of
expressing their gratitude and acknowledging the Pope's
help and protection."

In an article in the *New York Times,* James Feron noted
forty years ago that Jewish historian Pinchas Lapide, after
two years of research, came to the conclusion that Pope
Pius XII deserved a memorial forest in the Judean hills with
860,000 trees, the number of Jewish lives saved through
papal efforts. He had obtained information from accounts
of survivors in Israel, from privately published accounts,
and from the archives of Yad Vashem. Indeed, the Church
was instrumental in saving more Jews than those saved
by all other institutions and organizations combined. The
Pope depended on the local clergy to thwart Hitler's extermination policy. "The book dramatizes one point above all
others," Feron states, "that the Pope's efforts were depen-
dent on the strength and heroism of his churches in each
country." Lapide traces the efforts of Roman Catholics
to save the Jews and quotes a variety of sources to indi-
cate that papal nuncios had received messages from the
Vatican to contest the deportation of Jews. Lapide tells
how Pope Pius XII sent his papal nuncio in Berlin to visit

Hitler in Berchtesgaden to plead for the Jews. That interview ended when Hitler smashed a glass at the nuncio's
feet. From Hitler's reaction the Pope was convinced that
public pronouncements would have sealed the fate of many
more Jews. After this incident, and in retaliation, Hitler
connived to kidnap Pope Pius XII.

Obviously during the war years, the Vatican, concerned
about the Pope's safety, took measures to counter schemes
of malice. In fact, Robert A. Graham, one of the four edi-
tors of the Vatican documents, wrote a two-part article,
"Did Hitler Want to Remove Pius XII from Rome?" In
this article written a quarter of a century ago and published in Italian by *Civiltà Cattolica* (1972) one finds
the historical evidence confirming the claim in the Milan
newspaper *Il Giornale* (July 5, 1998).

References also appear in the memoirs, depositions,
and testimonies of diplomats and military leaders such as
Ulrich von Hassell, Ernst von Weizsäker, Robert M. W.
Kempner, Eitel Friedrich Moellhausen, and Rudolf Rahn.
Even Goebbels, Bormann, and others among Hitler's most
intimate associates were aware of the plot, as well as
officials of the SS, such as Eugenio Dollmann, Walter
Schellenberg, and Karl Wolff.

Some years ago Dan Kurzman interviewed Karl Wolff.
The general explained that Adolf Hitler called him into
his office on September 13, 1943, and spoke about his
relationship with Eugenio Pacelli, which dated back to

when he first came to power in 1933, and the bitter contempt that still existed between them. Reading from his own notes, Wolff quoted Hitler's words: "I have a special mission for you, Wolff. I want you and your troops to occupy Vatican City as soon as possible, secure its files and art treasures, and take the Pope and Curia to the north. I do not want him to fall into the hands of the Allies or to be under their political pressure and influence. The Vatican is already a nest of spies and a center of anti–National Socialist propaganda." This story is told in Kurzman's book *A Special Mission: Hitler's Secret Plot to Seize the Vatican and Kidnap Pope Pius XII* (Boston: DaCapo Press, 2007).

When he was elected on March 2, 1939, Pope Pius XII had the advantage of his knowledge of Germany, the German language, and the German people in his evaluation of the world situation. His words and actions bear testimony to his human qualities: he was a careful diplomat. The major consideration that he expressed repeatedly in his messages to the nuncios was to save lives. Albrecht von Kessel, aide-de-camp to Baron von Weizsäcker, the German ambassador, stated: "The members of the German embassy at the Vatican were at one in assessing the situation. A flaming protest on the part of Pius XII against the persecution of the Jews would presumably have put him and with him the Curia into extreme danger but would certainly . . . not have saved the life of a single Jew. Hitler, the animal of prey at bay, would react all the more cruelly the more resistance he met."

Ulrich von Hassell, in *The von Hassell Diaries: The Story of the Forces against Hitler Inside Germany, 1938–44,* provides the day-by-day testament of a leader of the anti-Nazi German resistance. He documents Pius XII's active assistance to the anti-Nazi cause within Germany and the esteem in which the Pontiff was held. Talks were arranged through the Pope for the purpose of laying a foundation for the discussion of peace terms after a change in the German regime. The confidential agent for Operation X was Dr. Josef Müller. Von Hassell records that a decision had been made in the event of the fall of Rome that "the Pope would be carried away for his own safety.... Our people are capable of this" (November 6, 1943).

3

Testimonials

Is Jewish Testimony Available?

Pope Pius XII sent many protests to the Nazis and saved thousands of Jewish lives, largely through diplomacy rather than confrontation. He knew that more explicit public condemnations would have continued to provoke brutal reprisals against the very people he was trying to help. He directed all the convents, monasteries, and churches to open their doors and hide Jews who otherwise would have been sent by the SS to the extermination camp in Auschwitz. According to a list compiled in 1963, by Italian historian Renzo DeFelice, Jewish refugees were hidden in 155 Catholic institutions in Rome. Mentioned are three convents and schools belonging to the Religious Teachers Filippini, where 114 Jews were saved. Mother Teresa Saccucci was interviewed during the war, and her memories are recorded in *La Chiesa e la Guerra (The Church and the War,* 1944). The Sisters helped the Holy Father in the Information Office of the Vatican Secretariat of State. Mother Teresa recalled: "For this work in the Information Office, I had designated five or six Sisters with typewriters. But every day there were other young women and children of the school who wanted to work for the Holy Father and answer the letters of prisoners of war and the needy. I did all I could to satisfy the Pope's wishes." Obviously, the work had to be kept secret. The Sisters dedicated themselves to this task.

In the archives of the Religious Teachers Filippini, who date back to 1692, there is a journal entry dated June 5, 1944: "Today began the exodus of the Jewish refugees. Over 60 women and children occupied the area designated for students, and also several rooms in the convent." The June 8, 1944, notation records that, following Vatican directives, these Sisters sponsored the "opening of a soup kitchen where the Sisters served meals to all refugees." In his own hand, Pius XII personally acknowledged the work of the Religious Teachers Filippini in Italy and in the United States of America. They assisted Pius XII as he cared for innocent civilians and racial groups targeted by Nazi persecution and was deeply involved in trying to save Jews.

During my trip to Rome in November 2006, I met with twenty-five Jews, relatives of a group of sixty Jews who lived in the convent of the Religious Teachers Filippini on Via delle Botteghe Oscure (also known as Via Arco de' Ginnasi, and Largo Santa Lucia Filippini) and thus were saved during the Nazi occupation of Rome in 1943. Many of their relatives are deceased, but several of those present said they remembered living in this convent when they were young. These Jews recognized the fact that the Sisters followed the instructions of the Pope. The following information is taken from notarized statements:

• Eleonora Perugia resides at Via G. Pession, 18, Rome. She was born on July 4, 1939. During the German occupation of Rome, she and her sister Elena, born November 12, 1941, were brought to this convent by their parents, who separated their seven children in order to save them from deportation. The two girls were entrusted to the Sisters until the end of the war.

• Davide Di Castro was born in Rome on November 23, 1938. He resides on Via Orti di Trastevere, 86. He declared that he was in his mother's arms when a member of the SS attacked her. Injured with the soldier's gun, he was brought to the hospital now known as Nuova Regina Margherita. Although he was not completely cured, he was dismissed because he was Jewish and the doctor was afraid of the Nazis. Thanks to these Sisters, he was cared for until the end of the war.

• Graziano Di Capua, who resides on Via Pagoda Bianca, 4, was born in Rome on January 13, 1939, when the racial laws were enacted in Italy. He was nine months old when he was afflicted with polio. No hospital would accept him because he was Jewish. When the deportations began, the young boy was taken to this convent, where he remained until the end of the war.

♦ Vittorio Polacco was born in Rome on January 26, 1941. He resides on Via Tuscolana, 713. On the morning of October 16, 1943, while living with his paternal grandparents in Rome, Lungotevere Ripa, 6, the Germans suddenly stormed their apartment and arrested him, his aunt and uncle, and his grandparents. They were placed in an open truck. Mrs. Assunta Fratini was passing by and recognized little Vittorio, the son of her neighbor. She made a sign to one of the prisoners on the truck who threw the little boy, as though he were a ball, into her arms when the guard turned away. She brought the little boy to her home on Via della Luce, 13. But when she saw other German soldiers approach the entrance, she knew she would be taking a risk if she kept the Jewish baby. She then went to her friend, Sister Lucia Mangone. The little boy remained in the convent after the end of the war although his parents were convinced he had been deported. Only when Mrs. Fratini later met his mother and asked about the little one did his parents learn what had happened.

♦ Elisabetta Moresco was born on August 18, 1939, and now resides on Via Bagno a Ripoli, 36, Rome. The family consisted of her parents and three children. Because of the racial laws enforced in Italy in 1938, her Jewish father lost his license as a merchant. When her parents were forced to escape to Norcia, they entrusted two children to Catholic families and brought their youngest daughter to the convent. Little Elisabetta remained away from her family until the end of the war. She continued to visit the Institution after the war and always remained close to Sister Margherita.

• Serafina Zarfati was born in Rome on April 30, 1934. She now resides in Rome on Via Francesco Arese, 15. In 1940 she could not attend public school because she was Jewish. The Jewish school in Rome was too distant from her home. So in 1940 she received tutoring from Sister Margherita Mita. Because of ill health, she was obliged to continue studies between 1941 and 1944 in the Convents of Nostra Signora di Sion and San Pancrazio. After the war, Serafina returned frequently to visit Sister Margherita.

• Elisabetta Di Tivoli was born February 27, 1943. She resides in Rome, Via Laura Mantegazza, 19. Her mother, Celeste Anticoli, delivered her baby prematurely. When Elisabetta was only two months old, because of the racial persecutions, she was entrusted to Sister Lucia Mangone and Sister Margherita Mita. There was no room for Celeste Anticoli in the convent, so she placed her baby in the arms of Sister Margherita and left. Undernourished and sickly, the child needed constant care. Hidden in the Roman hills, her parents lived in poverty. At the end of the war they returned for Elisabetta, who was now a year old and the child did not recognize her mother. She wanted to remain in the arms of Sister Margherita. Because the baby was so attached to Sister, Celeste Anticoli returned often to the convent and occasionally even had to let her daughter sleep there. To express their gratitude, the Di Tivoli family joined other Jews who were saved and collected funds in order to purchase a beautiful statue of Our Lady of Fatima for the Sisters.

• Mario Mieli was born in Rome on April 20, 1941. He and his parents lived with his maternal grandparents on Via Portico d'Ottavia, 10. During the Nazi roundup of October 16, 1943, the entire family, except his maternal grandmother, was arrested. Mario was saved, thanks to a Catholic neighbor who pretended she was the baby's mother. She saved him from deportation and entrusted him to the Sisters. Later his maternal aunt, Enrica Di Segni, adopted him. The entire family was deported and did not return.

• Ornella Della Torre was born October 31, 1941, in Rome, Via Virginia Agnelli, 100. Because of the racial laws enacted in 1938, Jews were deprived of all rights. Letizia Zarfati, her mother, was pregnant and ready to give birth. When she arrived at the hospital, she was refused admittance because she was Jewish. Fortunately she turned to the Sisters who assisted with the birth. When Ornella became very ill with whooping cough, the Sisters transferred her to their convent on Via delle Fornaci, just below the Gianicolo where she could breath fresh air. Later, because of her health, she was cared for in their convent on Via Sangemini (Monte Mario), where she remained until the end of the war.

◆ Silvana Di Veroli, who resides in Rome, Via Monte delle Capre, 10, was born on September 14, 1942. Because of the racial laws enforced in Italy in 1938, her Jewish father lost his position. To assure their children of the necessary sustenance and care, their parents sent Silvana and her twin sister, Enrica, to the convent of the Religious Teachers Filippini, located on Via Sangemini (Monte Mario).

In 1995, I interviewed several of the Sisters whose names are mentioned in these testimonials. Their accounts may be found in my book *Yours Is a Precious Witness: Memoirs of Jews and Catholics in Wartime Italy* (Paulist Press, 1997). An eyewitness was Sister Domenica Mitaritonne, who declared in a letter of September 26, 2000, that she resided in the Religious Teachers Filippini Convent at Via Caboto, 16, in the Ostiense Quarter of Rome: "Having received orders from the Holy Father, we welcomed the families of Jews who sought refuge from the Nazis and Fascists. Each night another Sister and I took turns watching through a window to see if the Germans were arriving in order to notify the Jews and help them hide under the stage in the little theater. One night we had a terrible scare when a German truck stopped nearby. We immediately alerted the Jews, who fled to safety. Fortunately, a neighbor had explained to the soldiers that this was an elementary school building and that there were no Jews living there."

Another eyewitness is Sister Maria Pucci, who prepared a notarized statement dated June 26, 2006. During the Nazi round-up, she lived in the same convent and witnessed the deportation of Jews as well as the bombing of the city of Rome. In her deposition she explains that it was Pope Pius XII who came to the rescue of the Jews. She states clearly that this convent and school were Vatican property and were supported by the Vatican. At the Pope's command to accept as many Jews as possible, they opened their doors, and thus thirty Jews were able to hide from the Nazis. They were treated as family while living in the convent and school. All were saved except two, seventy-year-old Attilio di Veroli and his sixteen-year-old son. One day they decided to go check the merchandise in their store and, despite the Sisters' insistence, they ventured out. Unfortunately, they were captured by the SS on the day preceding the Fosse Ardeatine Massacre and became victims of that German atrocity.

In gratitude to the Sisters, the Jews in Rome presented a beautifully decorated testimonial, which reads: "Whoever saves one life...it is as though he had saved the whole world (Sanhedrin IV, 5). The Jewish Community of Rome to the Religious Teachers Filippini, Via Caboto, Rome, recalling how they risked their own lives to save Jews from the nazi-fascist atrocities."

Did Pope Pius XII help the Jews? Indeed he did, directly and indirectly. Nor can one claim he was "silent." Rather one must speak of his "prudence." Almost fifty years have passed since Angelo Giuseppe Roncalli, apostolic nuncio in Istanbul, after an audience with Pope Pius XII on October 10, 1941, wrote in his *Diary* that the Pope's statements were "prudent." In 1958, three months after Pius XII's death, Pope John XXIII stated in his first Christmas message that his predecessor was worthy of canonization. In fact, a prayer with the *imprimatur* of Bishop Peter Canisius, vicar general of Vatican City, was circulated among the faithful. It stated that "Pius XII was a fearless defender of the faith, a valiant champion of justice and peace, a shining example of charity and all virtues."

4

Four Hundred Visas
Did Pius XII Obtain Them?

A marvelous glimpse into the way Pope Pius XII worked to help the persecuted Jews during the Holocaust may be found in my book *Consensus and Controversy.* Among the thousands of Jews saved directly by Pope Pius XII in 1942, there was one group of four hundred. Writing to the author on March 19, 2001, Monsignor Giovanni Ferrofino, an eyewitness and participant, tells the story, "Four Hundred Visas for Jews." Archbishop Maurilio Silvani (1882–1946), the titular archbishop of Lepanto, who was named nuncio to the Dominican Republic by Pius XII, May 23, 1942, is the papal representative who followed the Pope's instructions to help these Jews.

In this letter to Margherita Marchione from Maussane-les-Alpilles, France, Monsignor Giovanni Ferrofino gave his personal testimony: "During the war, I was at Port-au-Prince as secretary to Silvani, who had collaborated with Pacelli in Bavaria when he was secretary of state and during negotiations on the concordat with Germany. In 1942, instructions came to Nuncio Silvani from Pius XII telling him to ask General Rafael Leonida Trujillo, dictator of the Dominican Republic, to grant four hundred visas to Jews. It was subsequently learned that these refugees had been refused admittance to the United States.

"Nuncio Silvani immediately consulted the Dominican ambassador in Port-au-Prince who said: 'Trujillo will never say *No* to the Pope. But it is well known that the only way one can ask for such a favor is *in person.*' However, this would be an overnight trip. The capital of Santo Domingo was some 80 difficult kilometers across rocky Haitian territory and then another 350 kilometers of rugged Dominican roads under a blazing sun. And the nuncio was not well, but he set out at once.

"I remember that trip like yesterday. It was traumatic. It would have been difficult at any time but with the nuncio's illness, an illness that would eventually lead to his death, every hour was torture. When we arrived in the capital, the foreign minister very kindly offered use of an official car. We found Trujillo on horseback inspecting the sugar cane plantations, the *cañaverales*. He was wearing his *Panama*. As he tipped his hat to us, he made a move to dismount. But the nuncio shouted: 'Oh, no, General, remain on your horse. You already know why I am here.'

"Trujillo smiled, nodded, and replied that he could not refuse the Pope. But he had conditions. The dictator told us: 'None of the four hundred can remain in the capital. They must live on the frontier and protect us from the clandestine immigration of Haitians. They will have land, houses, everything that is needed for a well-organized colony.'

"We sent this information to the Vatican and returned to Haiti. A few weeks later, the four hundred Jews arrived in Santo Domingo. It was not long after they were settled that a taxi from the Dominican capital came to the nuncio's residence in Port-au-Prince. A couple stepped out of the taxi, identified themselves as two of the refugees, and asked to see Nuncio Silvani."

Ferrofino describes the meeting: "The couple thanked us and begged us to help them remain in Port-au-Prince. The wife was an attractive blond, ex-ballerina from the Vienna Opera House. The nuncio asked: 'What would you do in the capital?' They replied: 'Start a ballerina school.' The nuncio commented: 'I am not the most qualified person to tell you how to appeal to Trujillo for help to start a classical ballet school. Furthermore, as everyone knows, you must first win him over personally or by paying taxes. Trujillo never just gives anything to beautiful women.'

"I observed the two of them. There was no reaction from either the husband or the wife. They seemed stunned. They thanked us and left. But three years later, the diplomatic corps and all the members of the upper crust were invited to the opening of a new ballet school named after Trujillo's daughter, Flor de Oro. As for the others in the group of four hundred, one night, after having obtained passports from Mexico, they left clandestinely for Cuba and from that country, after a short stay there, they crossed the Mexican border and arrived safely in the United States, the land that had originally denied their entrance. All this happened, thanks to Pius XII."

These Jews were certainly aware that Pius XII had provided the necessary funds for their trip as well as the visas for Santo Domingo. The fact remains that of the four hundred Jews with visas, only the ballerina and her husband remained. The others crossed the Mexican border and arrived in the United States of America. Will Yad Vashem declare Pius XII "Righteous Among the Nations"?

It is also interesting to note that on September 19, 1942, Monsignor Paolo Bertoli, chargé d'affaires at Port-au-Prince, wrote to Cardinal Luigi Maglione, Vatican secretary of state, informing him that General Trujillo was ready to offer hospitality to thirty-five hundred Jewish children in France between the ages of three and fourteen. General Trujillo would organize the group and take care of expenses for their voyage. Again, thanks to Pius XII's intercession.

Archbishop Maurilio Silvani was later appointed papal nuncio to Chile. He sent a copy of letter No. 1261 on August 29, 1943, and stated: "The President of the 'Comité representativo de la Colectividad Israelita de Chile' begged me, on the 27th of this month, to send to the august Pontiff the expression of their gratitude for all that His Holiness is doing in defense of the Jews in

France and during the course of this war." From Santiago, the nuncio also sent a letter dated October 5, 1943, to Cardinal Maglione with a copy of the October 3 *El diario ilustrado* which he received from the president of the Committee, Samuele Goren. The article states: "During these tragic times our thoughts turn to the noble figure of the Supreme Pontiff, His Holiness Pius XII, proven defender of the cause of the persecuted and especially the millions of our European brothers and sisters who are the innocent victims of inhuman massacres and cruel abuse."

The Evian Conference was held in France in 1938. This international conference considered what to do about growing numbers of Jewish refugees fleeing Germany and Austria. It concluded that the Dominican Republic was the only country in the world that agreed to accept Jewish refugees as permanent residents. This story is documented by reporter Walter Ruby in an article that appeared in *The Jewish Week* of September 29, 2006. It has been confirmed by Oisiki Ghitis, religious director of the Jewish community in the Dominican Republic, who also stated that an Austrian-Jewish ballerina named Herta Brawer did indeed have a ballet school in Ciudad Trujillo during the Second World War.

5

Documentation

When Will Vilification of Pius XII End?

In a report filed with the U.S. State Department in 1939, Alfred W. Klieforth, U.S. consul general in Berlin, after a three-hour meeting "to discuss the situation in Germany," described Cardinal Pacelli's views: "He opposed unilaterally every compromise with National Socialism. He regarded Hitler not only as an untrustworthy scoundrel but as a fundamentally wicked person. He did not believe Hitler capable of moderation, in spite of appearances, and he fully supported the German bishops in their anti-Nazi stand."

Documents make clear that Pius XII told the Allies in late 1942 that he was prepared to issue a flaming explicit denunciation against both the Nazis and Soviet atrocities. However, because the Soviets were part of the Allied front against Nazism, the Allies immediately realized that any papal statement that included a condemnation of Soviet war crimes might fray the alliance and damage the anti-Nazi war effort. The Allies dropped their request.

Instead, the Pope included a clear statement against the Final Solution in his 1942 Christmas message.

In his classic work on the Holocaust, *Harvest of Hate,* Jewish historian Leon Poliakov writes that it is "certain" that the Vatican sent secret instructions to Europe's wartime bishops to protect Jews. This is underscored in a captured wartime Nazi document that rages against a Ukrainian bishop "for making the same statements and even using the same phrases as the French, Belgian and Dutch bishops, as if all of them were receiving the same instructions from the Vatican."

Dr. Joseph Lichten, a Polish-Jewish survivor of the Holocaust and official of the Anti-Defamation League, wrote in *A Question of Judgment: Pius XII and the Jews* (1963): "It is known that in 1940, Pius XII sent out a secret instruction to the Catholic bishops of Europe entitled *Opere et caritate* (By work and love), ordering that 'all people suffering from racial discrimination at the hands of the Nazis be given adequate help....' The letter was to be read in churches with the comment that racism was incompatible with the teachings of the Catholic faith."

As early as the autumn of 1940, shortly after Italy entered the war, Pius XII sent explicit instructions to the bishop of Salerno, Giuseppe Palatucci, to assist Jews in Campagna who had been interned by Mussolini's Fascist regime. The Pope accompanied his order with Vatican money for the suffering Jews.

Professor Ronald Rychlak, referring to sworn depositions in favor of Pius XII's beatification, commented: "The original transcripts take up just over 1,700 pages which are spread over seven volumes.... The clear message from each and every witness is that Eugenio Pacelli — Pius XII — was an honest, holy and charitable man — even saintly."

On December 18, 2006, Margherita Marchione sent documentation to Cardinal Camillo Ruini, Pope Benedict XVI's vicar for the City of Rome, relating to the present controversy surrounding Pope Pius XII. Dated January 3, 2007, Cardinal Ruini responded: "Notwithstanding all the opposition, the Cause for Beatification of Pius XII will proceed."

On Yad Vashem's website (*www.yadvashem.org*) there is an entry that appears in the *Encyclopedia for the Holocaust:* "In many monasteries, churches, and ecclesiastical buildings in Italy, Jews were saved during the Nazi occupation, and the simultaneous opening of many Catholic institutions could have taken place only under clear instructions by Pius XII. Moreover, the Pope protested officially, if only privately, against the persecution of the Jews in those countries where he felt that he might have some influence."

In the June 26, 1981, issue of the *Osservatore della Domenica,* Cardinal Paolo Dezza, S.J., summarized a very confidential report of an audience with Pope Pius XII. Referring to a retreat he gave for the Holy Father in the Vatican during the month of December 1942, he stated: "On that occasion I had a long audience in which Pius XII, speaking about the Nazi atrocities in Germany and in the other occupied countries, manifested his sorrow, his anguish. He said: 'They lament that the Pope does not speak. But the Pope cannot speak. If he were to speak, things would be worse.' And he reminded me that he had recently sent three letters in which he deplored the Nazi atrocities: one to the person he defined as 'the heroic archbishop of Cracow,' the future Cardinal Sapieha, and the others to two bishops in Poland. 'They responded,' he said, 'thanking me, but telling me that they could not publish those letters because it would aggravate the situation.' And he cited the example of Pius X who, when confronted with a problem in Russia, said: 'You must keep silence in order to avoid worse evils.'

"And even on this occasion, the inaccuracy of those who say that he kept silence because he wanted to support the Nazis against the Russians and Communism appears very clear. I recall that he told me: 'Yes, the danger of Communism exists; however, at this moment the danger of Nazism is greater.' And he spoke to me about what the Nazis would do if they were victorious. I remember he used the phrase: 'They want to destroy the Church and crush her like a toad. For the Pope there will be no place in the new Europe. They say that he should go to America. But I am not afraid, and I shall remain here.' And he said this in a very firm and sure manner so that one could clearly understand that if the Pope kept silence, it was not for fear or personal interest, but only just for fear of aggravating the situation of the oppressed. While speaking to me about the threats of invasion of the Vatican, he was absolutely tranquil, certain, trusting in Providence. Speaking to me about speaking out, he was full of anguish. 'If I speak,' he felt, 'I shall harm them.'

"Therefore, even if historically one could discuss whether it would have been better to speak more or speak more strongly, what is beyond discussion is that if Pope Pius XII did not speak more strongly it was purely for this reason, not for fear or any other interest.

"The other part of the conversation that impressed me was that he spoke about all he had done and was doing to help the oppressed. I recall that he spoke about the first steps he attempted to make, in agreement with the German cardinals, but with no results; then about the conversations he had with Ribbentrop when he came to Rome, but with no results. At any rate he continued to do whatever he could. His one preoccupation was to avoid entering into political or military questions and to remain within the sphere of that which was the duty of the Holy See. In this regard, I recall that when the Germans occupied Rome in 1943 (I was rector of the Pontifical Gregorian University, and it was I who accepted the refugees), Pius XII said to me: 'Father, avoid accepting the military because, since the Gregoriana is a pontifical house and belongs to the Holy See, we must be out of politics. But for

the others, help them willingly: poor, persecuted Jews.' "
Note that the Pope distinguished between military per-
sonnel and persecuted Jews. In fact, while the Jews were
accepted at the Gregoriana, the military were given sanctuary at Palazzo Callisto. Pius XII inspired his followers
to comfort suffering humanity and assist all war victims.

Pope Pius XII had served as the papal nuncio in Munich
and Berlin. After the war, when the Communists in Russia
began calumniating Pius XII in their newspaper *Izves-
tia*, Msgr. Fulton J. Sheen responded immediately in the
New York Times. The KGB wanted to depict the Pontiff
as an anti-Semite who had encouraged Hitler's Holocaust. Recently Lieutenant General Ion Mihai Pacepa, the
highest-ranking intelligence officer ever to have defected
from the former Soviet bloc, explained this issue in his
book *Red Horizons*, which has been published in twenty-
seven countries. Here he acknowledges that he was at
the center of Moscow's foreign intelligence wars and was
caught up in a deliberate Kremlin effort to smear the Vatican by portraying Pope Pius XII as a coldhearted Nazi
sympathizer.

In his opening speech during the prosecution of Adolf
Eichmann on April 17, 1961, Attorney General Gideon
Hausner stated: "When the Pope himself interceded for
the Jews of Rome and Eichmann was asked to leave
them in Italian labor camps instead of deporting them,
the request was turned down. The Jews were sent to
Auschwitz."

Witnesses honored by Yad Vashem as "Righteous Among the Nations" have come forward to state unequivocally that Pius XII gave direct and explicit instructions, both verbal and written, to his assistants and nuncios, to do everything they could to save Jews.

Regarding the rescue of Jews by Catholic institutions in Rome, Father David Jeager, an Israeli-born convert to Catholicism and an expert on Vatican canon law, stated: "Anyone who has any acquaintance with the laws and culture of the Catholic Church at that time would understand those things could not have taken place without specific orders of the Pope, and those orders could not have been in written form."

6

World Press

How Has the Press Responded?

Newspapers throughout the world acknowledged Pope Pius XII's efforts on behalf of persecuted Jews during World War II. No one can deny that during the period of the Holocaust Pius XII spoke out against Nazism! His voice was indeed heard. There is documentation available in the archives of the Vatican Radio, *L'Osservatore Romano,* the London *Times,* the *Tablet* of London, and the *New York Times.* Throughout World War II, Pius XII continually attacked Nazi policies. He so provoked the Nazis that they called him "a mouthpiece of the Jewish war criminals."

There were sixty Vatican dispatches to Berlin protesting Adolf Hitler's treatment of the Jews before World War II. How can anyone claim that Cardinal Pacelli "said and did nothing" after Hitler began violating the concordat and savagely persecuted Jews?

Before the 1933 concordat with Germany, the SS and Gestapo had rounded up and incarcerated thousands of supporters and activists of the leading Catholic Center

Party and were threatening thousands more. The former Chancellor, Heinrich Brüning, stated that Catholic youth leaders had already been tortured to death, and there was a ghastly fate hanging over others. By signing a concordat, which might give legal protection and accord a semblance of civil rights to those already imprisoned, Cardinal Eugenio Pacelli (the future Pope Pius XII) was following the most admirable principles of Christian charity. He could not foretell the demonic paths Nazism was to tread in the following years.

The struggle against the Church did, in fact, become ever more bitter; there was the dissolution of Catholic organizations; the gradual suppression of the flourishing Catholic schools, both public and private; the enforced weaning of youth from family and Church; the pressure brought to bear on the conscience of citizens and especially of civil servants; the systematic defamation, by means of a clever, closely organized propaganda, of the Church, the clergy, the faithful, the Church's institutions, teaching, and history; the closing, dissolution, and confiscation of religious houses and other ecclesiastical institutions; the complete suppression of the Catholic press and publishing houses.

By 1935, the Vatican was complaining about "German non-fulfillment of its terms and also protesting against pagan elements in the Nazi ideology, such as the doctrine of racism and the persecution of the Jews. . . . During the Nazi reign of terror in the city (of Rome) after the overthrow of Mussolini, substantial numbers of escaped prisoners of war, Jews and leaders of democratic parties were sheltered by the ecclesiastical power" (*Encyclopaedia Britannica,* 1962).

On May 12, 1941, the Vatican asked the British government to facilitate visits by papal representatives to prison camps. A few days later, on May 19, 1941, the Pope renewed his efforts to obtain lists of prisoners of war. Again, on September 25, 1941, there was a formal request for intervention in order to obtain information about prisoners of war in Russia. There was also a memorandum on Vatican efforts to promote the exchange of sick and maimed prisoners (March 1, 1943) and the repatriation of Italian prisoners of war (March 11, 1943).

Among the many requests for information, a document dated March 12, 1943, regards the need for an investigation on behalf of Jews in Poland threatened with extermination. Activities of the Holy See on behalf of prisoners in Russian hands and Russian prisoners are repeated: "Finding it impossible to render any other assistance to prisoners of war in Russian hands, the Holy See concentrated its efforts in seeking to obtain lists of these prisoners and in trying to establish a news service between them and their respective families. To this end representations were made to the governments of the United States, Great Britain, and Sweden, and the apostolic delegates of London, Washington, Teheran, and Istanbul were also requested to use their influence for the same purpose."

On March 1, 2000, the Israeli government released Adolf Eichmann's *Diary*, describing the extermination of Jews by the Nazi regime and the actions taken by Pope Pius XII when Jews in Rome were deported on October 16, 1943. Eichmann clearly states that the Vatican "vigorously protested the arrest of Jews, requesting the interruption of such action; to the contrary, the Pope would denounce it publicly." These memoirs reveal the truth.

There is documentary evidence that Nazis had only contempt for Pius XII and ridiculed him even when he was secretary of state. Indeed, cartoons appearing in propaganda articles depict Pius as a co-conspirator with Jewish and Communist elements, acting to destroy National Socialism. He is drawn with grotesque "Jewish" features. If the Nazis could have pointed to the figure of the Pope as a secret sympathizer, it would have been an immense propaganda coup for the Third Reich at the time. With the combined forces of the United States, the Soviet Union, and Great Britain against Germany, the need to boost morale was compelling and desperate. Had Pius XII stridently protested, more lives would have been lost. Jewish scholar Jenö Levai, testifying at the Adolf Eichmann Nazi war crime trials, insisted that bishops of the Catholic Church "intervened again and again on the instructions of the Pope.... The one person who did more than anyone else to halt the dreadful crime and alleviate its consequences, is today made the scapegoat for the failures of others."

Judge Joseph Proskauer, president of the American Jewish Committee, stated: "We have seen how great was the work of the Holy Father in saving the Jews in Italy. We also learned from various sources that this great Pope has tried to help and save the lives of Jews in Hungary." According to Mary Ann Glendon, professor of law at Harvard University, "The tragedy of the Jewish people has been shamelessly exploited by foes of traditional religion."

An unpublished document among apostolic delegate Angelo Roncalli's notes (Istanbul, June 1944) contradicts the statements by Tel Aviv University professor Dina Porat that Pius XII failed to do all he could to prevent the massacre of Jews. The facts show that Roncalli met Chaim Barlas, secretary of the Jewish Agency for Palestine, on June 27, not on June 24. This proves that Pius XII intervened in favor of the Hungarian Jews before Barlas spoke to Roncalli. In fact, on August 18, 1944, Roncalli wrote to Ira A. Hirschmann that the only way to help was through the secretary of state, and he assured him that the Vatican had done and was doing its very best. There was no mention of disagreement between Roncalli and Pius XII. As honorary consul general in Milan, Pinchas Lapide wrote: "When I was received by Roncalli in Venice, I expressed the gratitude of my country for his help while in Turkey. He interrupted me repeatedly to remind me that he always followed Pius XII's directives" (*Le Monde*, December 1963).

Chief Rabbi Joseph Hertz in London had written to the delegate, Monsignor William Godfrey, on March 22, 1944: "The very serious turn of events in Hungary renders the plight of the Jews in that country perilous in the extreme, and only the urgent intervention of His Holiness the Pope can save hundreds of thousands of human lives from the horrors that befell them in Rumania and Poland. As chief rabbi, I earnestly appeal for such intervention. The lay leaders of my community, as well as the Executive of the National Committee for Rescue from the Nazi Terror, wholeheartedly associate themselves in this appeal through you to His Holiness."

Godfrey transmitted the request to the Vatican on March 30: "The Holy See has been concerned about the fate of the Jewish residents in Hungary and has already appealed in this regard to the apostolic nuncio in Budapest even though one does not have too much hope." The delegate informed the chief rabbi of Maglione's response (April 4). Hertz immediately thanked him (April 10).

Later, the British legation to the secretariat of state sent a request for intervention on behalf of Hungarian Jews: "It is hoped that the Holy See, in accordance with the principle of universal charity, will exercise such influence as they can to protect Jewish refugees in Hungary from being handed over to the German authorities. It is understood that the influence of His Holiness has in the past been very effective in this matter, but it is appreciated that in changing circumstances action may be more difficult. In any case any action in this sense that it may be found feasible to take will be highly appreciated" (April 1, 1944).

The secretariat of state responded to the legation on April 5, 1944: "The Holy See has renewed its earnest request with regard to the fate of the Jewish residents in Hungary through the apostolic nuncio in Budapest." The London branch of Agudas Israel World Organisation was informed by Monsignor Godfrey of the efforts by the Holy See on behalf of the Jews in Hungary. They thanked the delegate on April 13.

In a telegram to Cardinal Maglione, July 21, 1944, the World Jewish Congress requested that His Holiness make a final appeal to regent Horthy to release Hungarian Jews, particularly children.

Already on June 25, 1944, Pius XII had telegraphed a personal protest message to Admiral Horthy, the regent in Budapest: "Supplications have been addressed to Us from different sources that we should exert all Our influence to shorten and mitigate the sufferings that have, for so long, been peacefully endured on account of their national or racial origin by a great number of unfortunate people belonging to this noble and chivalrous nation. In accordance with Our service of love, which embraces every human being, Our fatherly heart could not remain insensible to these urgent demands. For this reason we apply to Your Serene Highness, appealing to your noble feelings in the full trust that Your Serene Highness will do everything in your power to save many unfortunate people from further pain and sorrow." Horthy stopped deportations almost immediately. He was arrested and imprisoned by the Nazis on October 15.

Y. Bankover "Hamèsh Shanìm," in *Diario di un soldato ebreo,* writes: "In the midst of the general destruction that characterized the war zones, Rome remained intact. 'A miracle took place here': thousands of Jews were safe and sound. The Church, the religious houses, monks, sisters and above all the Pontiff, have worked in an extraordinary way to save Jews from the clutches of the Nazis and their collaborators, the Italian Fascists. While endangering their own lives, they succeeded with great efforts in hiding and feeding the Jews during the German occupation of Rome. Some religious paid the price with their lives to accomplish this (Don Pietro Pappagallo and Don Giuseppe Morosini). The entire Church participated with devotion in this effort. Not less important and decisive in saving lives was the help given by the population of Rome. The citizens generally hid Jews in their homes, feeding them with the little food they had. Every Jewish family that returned home after the Germans left, found their own house in order, thanks to the Christian citizens, notwithstanding the dangers encountered, who guarded the homes of the Jews under the very eyes of the Gestapo."

The following communication is from Captain Efraim Urbach, rabbi-chaplain of the Eighth British Army, to Dr. Leo Cohen, director general of the political department of the Jewish Agency, Jerusalem: "With this letter I send you the first summary on the conditions of the Jews of Rome, as I have witnessed after my one day visit.... Persons of the Church have helped Jews and hid women and children, within the limits that were possible."

Captain Urbach wrote: "Following up on what I have already communicated with my preceding letter, I now give you some particulars.... This work of assistance must be attributed to the Persons of the Church. In a special way German Father Weber of the Pallottine Fathers and Capuchin Father Benedetto distinguished themselves. Many Jews were hidden in convents." These statements come from the Zionist Central Archives in Jerusalem.

Sergeant Yechiel Duvdevano was among the most influential heads of the Zionist Movement and of the Hagana organization of defense. In the years 1943–45 he coordinated the assistance given to Jews in the Italian regions that were liberated. "... Jews remained hidden, with Christian names, for 9 months, in cellars and in catacombs. Many found refuge in convents; especially children.... The Germans promised a reward for every

Jew that was captured and presented to them.... The main help came from the Church."

On August 2, 1943, the Jewish Congress sent the following message to Pope Pius XII: "World Jewish Congress respectfully expresses gratitude to Your Holiness for your gracious concern for innocent peoples afflicted by the calamities of war and appeals to Your Holiness to use your high authority by suggesting Italian authorities may remove as speedily as possible to southern Italy or other safer areas twenty thousand Jewish refugees and Italian nationals now concentrated in internment camps...and so prevent their deportation and similar tragic fate which has befallen Jews in Eastern Europe. Our terror-stricken brethren look to Your Holiness as the only hope for saving them from persecution and death."

The following month four thousand Jews and Yugoslav nationals who had been in internment camps were removed to an area that was under the control of Yugoslav partisans. As such, they were out of immediate danger. The report went on to say: "The Jews concerned will probably not yet know by what agency their removal from danger has been secured, but when they do they will be indeed grateful."

Two months later, Rabbi Herzog again wrote to Pope Pius XII expressing his "sincere gratitude and deep appreciation for so kind an attitude toward Israel and for such valuable assistance given by the Catholic Church to the endangered Jewish people." Jewish communities in Chile,

Uruguay, and Bolivia also sent similar offers of thanks to the Pope.

Measures were taken by Pope Pius XII to save all victims of the Nazis. Dramatic evidence has surfaced in an article by Marco Tosatti (*La Stampa*, August 8, 2006). It reaffirms what has long been known but denied by critics: the Pope ordered religious convents and monasteries to open their doors to shelter political fugitives and Jews during World War II. Tosatti's article describes the journal of an Augustinian nun in the convent of Santi Quattro Coronati in Rome. This documentation has been published by the magazine *30Days*. It is a newly discovered Holocaust diary that reveals the drastic steps taken by the Pope and the Catholic Church to save the lives of Jews and others being hunted down by the Nazis.

According to the journal, Pius XII instructed the mother superior to allow those fleeing from the Germans to enter the cloistered convent and remain as long as necessary. Not only does the Augustinian author provide details, but she explains that the Pope wished to save "the children as well as Jews" and ordered that monasteries and enclosures should be opened to protect those persecuted. She admits she prepared false identity papers for all her guests. "Unfortunately," the nun writes, "with the coming of the Germans in September, the war against the Jews — whom they wish to exterminate with the most barbarous atrocities — included young Italians and political activists who were tortured and subjected to the most horrible sufferings.... We adhered to the wishes of the Holy Father."

Personally and through his representatives, Pius XII employed all the means at his disposal to save Jews and other refugees during World War II. As a moral leader and a diplomat forced to limit his words, he privately took action and, despite insurmountable obstacles, saved hundreds of thousands of Jews from the gas chambers.

Kenneth L. Woodward wrote in *Newsweek:* "No one person, Hitler excepted, was responsible for the Holocaust. And no one person, Pius XII included, could have prevented it. In choosing diplomacy over protest, Pius XII had his priorities straight. It's time to lay off this pope" (March 30, 1998).

Pius XII was concerned that a public condemnation would result in retaliation and the loss of more lives. His "silence" accompanied a powerful action in defense of the Jews: he opened the very doors of the Vatican for thousands of Jews to hide there. In obedience to the Pope's directives, 155 ecclesiastical institutions welcomed thousands of Jews and other refugees whose lives were saved during the Nazi occupation of Rome.

It is irresponsible to deprive future generations of the contemporary assessments and judgments that together comprise part of the historical record of the Holocaust era. British historian Sir Martin Gilbert stated: "So the test for Pacelli was when the Gestapo came to Rome in 1943 to round up Jews. And the Catholic Church, on his direct authority, immediately dispersed as many Jews as they could." Gilbert's *Never Again: The History of the Holocaust* contains an extraordinary chapter on Pope Pius XII, whose protection of refugees and victims of persecution was one of the finest examples of Christian charity.

On January 25, 2007, speaking at a conference to mark the publication of the Italian translation of Gilbert's *The Righteous: The Unsung Heroes of the Holocaust,* Vatican secretary of state Cardinal Tarcisio Bertone strongly defended Pope Pius XII against critics who charge that the Pontiff failed to protect Jews during the Holocaust: "Research done by independent historians confirm that Pope Pius XII took extraordinary steps to save Jewish lives." With reference to the Church's intervention, Cardinal Bertone pointed out: "It is clear that Pope Pacelli was not about silence but about intelligent and strategic speaking, as demonstrated in the 1942 Christmas radio message, which infuriated Hitler. The proofs are in the Vatican archives."

In an interview by Andrea Tornielli for the Italian newspaper *Il Giornale,* Sir Martin Gilbert commented: "As a Jewish historian, I have felt the need to fully recognize the help given by Catholics to Jews during the Second World War.... Priests and bishops saved Jews wherever they were threatened, including Poland, France, and Italy.... The Nazis recognized the fact that Pope Pius XII directed his representatives to save the persecuted Jews by opening the doors of Catholic institutions. They considered Pope Pius XII an enemy of Germany." The point the author made about the kidnapping of the Pope was that it would have had disastrous consequences for Catholics throughout the area under German rule.

7

Jewish Survivors

Have Survivors Acknowledged Help?

Testimonials of survivors of the Holocaust make it perfectly clear that the Pope was not anti-Semitic or indifferent to the fate of the Jews and that he did everything possible to help them. On October 10, 1958, the day after Pius XII's death, Mark Segal, a reporter for the *Jerusalem Post,* interviewed Prof. Guido Mendes, a childhood friend and classmate of Eugenio Pacelli. Their paths separated when Pacelli entered the seminary and Mendes studied medicine. He became a lung specialist and, when interviewed, was living in Ramat Gan: "In 1938, with the beginning of the persecution of the Italian Jews, Pacelli's secretary called from the Vatican to ask the Mendes family if they needed help. The Mendes family later escaped to Switzerland, and the Vatican secured them certificates to Palestine. . . . Mr. Mendes recalled that the Pope, meeting survivors of the concentration camps in Italy in 1945, had then predicted *soon, you will have a Jewish state.*"

Documentation shows that when Jews were threatened by racial laws in Italy, Vatican secretary of state Eugenio Pacelli ordered Giovanni Montini (the future Pope Paul VI) to provide the means for Jewish surgeon Guido Mendes to emigrate with his entire family. Guido had been his schoolmate at the Ennio Quirino Visconti Lyceum in Rome. The friendship between them was still vivid in 1958 in the elderly Mendes's memory when he described Eugenio as a careful dresser, always wearing a coat and tie and distinguishing himself as the leading student. "He was always winning academic prizes," Mendes recalled. He also stated that when the Fascists began to threaten Jews in Italy, the then secretary of state Pacelli helped the Mendes family flee from Italy. They remained in touch with one another over the years.

During this period of persecution, in response to Benito Mussolini's anti-Jewish legislation, Pius XII appointed several Jewish scholars to important positions inside the Vatican. In fact, his first encyclical, *Summi Pontificatus,* expressly mentioned the Jews, noting that in the Catholic Church there is "no longer Greek and Jew, circumcised and uncircumcised, barbarian, Scythian, slave and free; but Christ is all and in all (Colossians 3:10–11)."

Among the many survivors is historian Michael Tagliacozzo. In a letter to me, dated June 18, 1997, this Holocaust survivor clearly expressed his sentiments: "In my study of the conditions of the Jews, I pointed out the generous and vast activity of the Church in favor of the victims. I learned how great was Pope Pacelli's paternal solicitude. No honest person can discount his merits.... Pacelli was the only one who intervened to impede the deportation of Jews on October 16, 1943, and he did very much to hide and save thousands of us. It was no small matter that he ordered the opening of cloistered convents. Without him, many of our own would not be alive."

Again, years later, in a letter of August 8, 2004, he reiterated his convictions: "Any apology on the actions of Pius XII must be considered superfluous. This is clear to all men of good will and is entrusted above all to the memory of those Jews, now living, who have not forgotten the efforts and solicitude of Pope Pacelli.... One must add the countless expressions of gratitude of those whose lives were saved in the religious houses in Rome, Assisi, and elsewhere. Even if gratitude was expressed directly to the institutions who protected them, the merit goes to Pope Pacelli who, on October 16, 1943, gave orders to open the doors of the parishes, convents, and monasteries to save the Jews from deportation."

Jews who survived in Rome as a result of Pius XII's directives have left us testimonials, interviews, and public acknowledgments toward the Pope, the Catholic Church, and its religious organizations.

Michael Tagliacozzo wrote a letter to the daily newspaper *Davàr,* which states: "Little known is the precious help of the Holy See. On the recommendation of Pius XII the religious of every order did their best to save Jews. In great numbers, especially the elderly, women, and children were welcomed in the convents that opened their doors offering refuge and assistance. Children in orphanages were sent to monasteries. Even in the Vatican, almost under the Pope's windows, Jews found refuge hiding from the clutches of the Gestapo" (Tel Aviv, April 23, 1985). The figures show that about 5,000 were hiding in ecclesiastical institutions; there were 4,238 living in convents, parishes, and other institutions, while 477 were living in the extraterritorial buildings protected by the Holy See.

L'Osservatore Romano (January 5, 1946) reported a statement by Reuben Resnick, American director of the Committee to Help Jews in Italy, declaring that "all the members of the Catholic hierarchy in Italy, from cardinals to priests, saved the lives of thousands of Jews, men, women, and children who were hosted and hidden in convents, churches, and other religious institutions."

Addressed to His Holiness Pope Pius XII, another article appeared in *L'Osservatore Romano* on April 5, 1946: "The delegates of the Congress of the Italian Jewish Communities, held in Rome for the first time after the Liberation, feel that it is imperative to extend reverent homage to Your Holiness, and to express the most profound gratitude that animates all Jews for your fraternal humanity toward them during the years of persecution when their lives were endangered by Nazi-Fascist barbarism. Many times priests suffered imprisonment and were sent to concentration camps, and offered their lives to assist Jews in every way. This demonstration of goodness and charity that still animates the just, has served to lessen the shame and torture and sadness that afflicted millions of human beings."

There were many demonstrations of thanks and gratitude from individual Jews saved through the assistance of Church institutions. Abramo Giacobbe Isaia Levi, a man of renowned intellect and a senator of the Kingdom of Italy until the promulgation of the racial laws, was hidden in a convent during the Nazi occupation of Rome. He and his wife later converted to Christianity. He died in 1949 and, in his will, left a large sum of money to help elderly and impoverished Italian Jews. His beautiful estate in the center of Rome, Villa Levi, was renamed Villa Giorgina, in memory of his young daughter who died prematurely. In his will Isaia Levi donated this estate to Pope Pius XII because he had been "preserved from the dangers of evil racial persecution," and was "grateful for the protection that was provided in that turbulent period by the Sisters of the Infant Mary."

8

The Bombing of Rome

Did the Pope Help Stop the Bombing?

During World War II, Pope Pius XII was in direct contact with Franklin Delano Roosevelt, president of the United States. Indeed, Roosevelt asked the Vatican to help overcome the American Catholics' opposition to his plan to grant Russia, then fighting Hitler, the support already being extended to Great Britain. His request was granted. The Vatican Secretariat of State then asked the apostolic delegate in Washington to direct the task of explaining to American bishops that henceforth the encyclical *Divini Redemptoris,* which ordered Catholics to refuse alliances with all the Communist parties, was not to apply to the present situation and did not forbid the American wartime help to Soviet Russia.

In response to Roosevelt's letter of December 31, 1942, during the most crucial moment in the war, on January 5, 1943, the Pope expressed his readiness to collaborate with him to achieve peace. "While maintaining this prayerful watch . . . it is Our undeviating program to do everything in Our power to alleviate the countless sufferings arising from this tragic conflict: sufferings of the prisoners and of the wounded, of families in fear and trembling over the fate of their loved ones, of entire peoples subjected to limitless privations and hardships; sufferings of the aged, of women and children who at a moment's notice find themselves deprived of home and possessions."

President Roosevelt wrote on August 3, 1944, to Myron C. Taylor, his personal representative: "I should like you to take the occasion to express to His Holiness my deeply felt appreciation of the frequent action which the Holy See has taken on its own initiative in its generous and merciful efforts to render assistance to the victims of racial and religious persecutions."

When the Allies bombed the ancient and priceless papal Basilica of San Lorenzo, on July 19, 1943, Pius XII appealed to President Roosevelt: "It is Our prayer that everywhere, as far as humanly possible, the civil populations be spared the horrors of war; that the homes of God's poor be not laid in ashes; that the little ones and youth, a nation's hope, be preserved from all harm — how Our heart bleeds when We hear of helpless children made victims of cruel war — that churches dedicated to the worship of God and monuments that enshrine the memory and masterpieces of human genius be protected from destruction."

While maintaining neutrality and impartiality consistent with the Holy See's policy regarding civil antagonisms between states, His Holiness expressed great pleasure that no vindictive motives were evident in the views of the United States and that, in the interest of permanent moral and peaceful relations, the welfare of all peoples would be protected and assured. He believed that the solution of postwar problems must be considered particularly in the light of the principle of the unity of mankind and of the family of peoples.

Although Pius XII begged the Allies to spare Rome and the Vatican, he did not succeed. The magazine *Ecclesia* records his charity during the bombing of Rome, when American bombers dropped tons of explosives on July 19, 1943. As bishop of Rome, he hastened to console and to comfort his people. When he learned that the Tiburtina section was bombed, hundreds were buried under the ruins, dead or injured, and the Church of San Lorenzo destroyed, he sent his secretary to withdraw all his personal funds from the bank, ordered his chauffeur to accompany him without the official escort, and hastened to the area. His white cassock was stained with the blood of those to whom he administered the Last Rites.

Again, on August 13, 1943, when the Allies bombed Rome near Appia Nuova and Tuscolana, the Pope rushed to the area and, as he distributed funds, he blessed and consoled his flock. A mother shoved her dead child into the Pope's arms while he tried to console her. Others begged for help, as he administered the Last Rites and comforted the injured. Among the victims was a little girl lying on a stretcher, cold and immobile. Kneeling beside her, the Pope touched the child and spoke to her. At the sound of his consoling voice, the child opened her eyes, got up, and walked away.

On November 5, 1943, Allied bombs fell not only on the Pope's summer estate in Castelgandolfo, but also on the Vatican and the city of Rome. In fact, the Pope's apartment in Castelgandolfo, as well as windows of the cupola of St. Peter's, were shattered. Also, the Vatican railroad station, the laboratory for mosaics, the Governatorato building, and the Church of Santa Marta were damaged. Pius XII's appeal for assistance and help for the poor in Italy was heeded by Catholics throughout the world. Among those who responded were members of the Religious Teachers Filippini in the United States.

It is to the credit of the American people that, with the active cooperation of the Vatican, a National Agency for the Distribution of Relief was formed to help millions of displaced peoples, prisoners of war, men and women engaged in forced labor away from their homelands, and civilian internees in all parts of Europe.

Cesare Carnevale, an eyewitness, wrote: "Pius XII was the Pope of my youth. I still recall the impression I had looking at this saintly figure in white with arms outstretched in prayer as everyone turned to him during the bombings of Rome. . . . But I also have a very personal memory. During the 1950s, I was a young Salesian priest in Grottaferrata and worked with the youth of the area.

We had a sports field but no equipment for the young-sters. So I turned directly to His Holiness and asked him to help me obtain sports equipment. Within a few days I received a large box with everything needed for a successful program: shirts, pants, shoes, footballs, soccer balls, etc."

Indeed, confirmation of a request for soccer balls to help children adjust in the aftermath of the war is found in a letter to Mother Ninetta Jonata in Morristown, New Jersey, dated June 18, 1947, from the Vatican secretary of state, asking for "footballs." This letter in the Archives of the Religious Teachers Filippini also acknowledges cases of supplies that had arrived from the United States: "29 cases on the ship *City of Athens;* 60 cases on the *Exiria;* 90 cases on the *Waimea.*"

During and after the war, in consonance with the Pope's wishes, not only did the Religious Teachers Filippini in the United States ship tons of cases of medicine and clothing to the Vatican, but they also visited the sequestered Italian prisoners of war and internees. The charity of helping the Pope care for the needy continued for about twenty years.

When this work of mercy was no longer possible, Sister Margherita Marchione crossed the Atlantic on the *Michelangelo* toward the end of May 1966 to accompany the last cases of clothing and medicines for the Pope's poor. The Religious Teachers Filippini followed Pius XII's directives to open the doors of their convents through-out Italy to hide Jews from the Nazis and Fascists. Many remained in these convents for about a year. At the end of the war, a group of Jews visited the Religious Teachers Filippini to express their thanks and offered them the gift of a five-foot statue of Our Lady of Fatima, which still stands on the fourth floor of the convent on Via delle Botteghe Oscure.

This charitable work of the Religious Teachers Filippini continued for many years after the war. On March 26, 1951, Pius XII wrote to Mother Ninetta: "We desire to express to you, beloved daughter, Our lively appreciation of the truly charitable spirit which animated you and those associated with you in the generous donation of relief supplies which you have forwarded to the Vatican. It is always a source of consolation to us to be reminded, through charitable acts such as yours, that Our children in America share Our great concern for the plight of those unfortunate souls who are living in circumstances of wretchedness and misery."

9

Nazis and Jews

Did Nazis and Jews Speak Out?

The Holocaust took place during a complex and dark period of human history. When will the indictment against the Church and, in particular, against Pius XII end? The Catholic Church was the only institution that had the courage to denounce the Nazi action during the Holocaust. Should historians ignore testimonials by Nikolaus Kunkel, Adolf Eichmann, Israel Zolli, Alexander Safran, Isaac Herzog, and many other Nazi and Jewish witnesses who defended the actions of Pope Pius XII?

Lieutenant Nikolaus Kunkel

On January 24, 2001, *L'Osservatore Romano* carried the testimony of a Nazi witness to Pius XII's actions to save Roman Jews during the Second World War. In an interview with the German Catholic News Agency (KNA), Nikolaus Kunkel, a lieutenant at the headquarters of the military governor of Rome in 1943, stated that he directly witnessed the SS roundup of the Jews.

He remembers those dramatic days when the SS wanted to take advantage of the transition of power from Mussolini to Badoglio to carry out "the final solution to the Jewish question."

When asked if he thought that a more vigorous protest from Pope Pius XII would have saved more Jews in Rome, Italy, and occupied Europe, Kunkel stated: "At the time I spoke about this with my immediate superior, Major Böhm, a Protestant from Hamburg. We were both of the opinion that, faced with Hitler's unpredictability, any action directed to world public opinion by the Pope would have been harmful.... Pius XII was in a most difficult political situation. Considering the circumstances, no one can reproach him for his actions." The SS unit's task was to deport all the Jews in Rome. According to Kunkel, "When the rumor of the raid proved to be true, Major General Rainer Stahel summoned and informed the officers of divisions 1A, 1B, and 1C saying that he was totally opposed to the operation."

Adolf Eichmann

The Nazi leader Adolf Eichmann was condemned to death in Jerusalem in 1961 for crimes against the Jewish people. He affirms the truth about the Holocaust and the undeniable evidence that exists and has been ignored regarding Pius XII's humanitarianism. His words confirm the thesis of those historians who have collected documents on the action undertaken by the Vatican to defend Jews. Eichmann states in his *Diary* that the Vatican "vigorously protested the arrest of Jews." Why did the Israeli government wait more than forty years to release this documentation?

The truth is also told in General Herbert Kappler's own words: "At that time, my office received the copy of a letter, that I immediately gave to my direct superiors, sent by the Catholic Church in Rome, in the person of Bishop Hudal, to the commander of the German forces in Rome, General Stahel. The Church was vigorously protesting the arrest of Jews of Italian citizenship, requesting that such actions be interrupted immediately throughout Rome and its surroundings."

On October 6, 1943, German ambassador Moellhausen sent a telegraphic message to Foreign Minister Joachim von Ribbentrop in which he said that General Kappler, SS commander in Rome, had received a special order from Berlin to arrest eight thousand Jews who were living in Rome and to deport them to northern Italy, where they would be exterminated. General Stahel, commander of the German forces in Rome, explained to Moellhausen that, from his point of view, it would be better to use the Jews for fortification works. On October 9, however, Ribbentrop answered that the eight thousand Jews of Rome had to be deported to the Mathausen concentration camp.

Eichmann wrote in his diary: "The objections given and the excessive delay in the steps necessary to complete the implementation of the operation resulted in a great part of Italian Jews being able to hide and escape capture."

Chief Rabbi Israel Zolli

An important witness to the role of Pius XII in wartime Italy is Rabbi Israel Zolli, chief rabbi of Rome during the Nazi occupation and persecution of Jews. A biblical scholar whose courage and integrity cannot be challenged, Rabbi Zolli was hidden in the Vatican. He was an eyewitness of the deportation of Rome's Jews by the Gestapo in 1943. He was converted to Catholicism and took the name Eugenio in Baptism in honor of Pius XII. In his book *Antisemitismo,* he states: "World Jewry owes a great debt of gratitude to Pius XII for his repeated and pressing appeals for justice on behalf of the Jews and, when these did not prevail, for his strong protests against evil laws and procedures." Zolli, who found shelter in the Vatican during the war, also stated: "No hero in all of history was more militant, more fought against, none more heroic than Pius XII in pursuing the work of true charity! . . . and this on behalf of all the suffering children of God."

Rabbi Zolli devoted an entire chapter to the German occupation of Rome in his 1954 memoirs, *Before the Dawn.* He praised the Pope's leadership during World War II: "The people of Rome loathed the Nazis and had intense pity for the Jews. They willingly assisted in the evacuation of the Jewish population into remote villages, where they were protected by Christian families.... The Holy Father sent by hand a letter to the bishops instructing them to lift the enclosure from convents and monasteries, so that they could hide the Jews. I know of one convent where the sisters slept in the basement, giving up their beds to Jewish refugees. In face of this charity, the fate of so many of the persecuted is especially tragic."

Chief Rabbi Alexander Safran

Chief Rabbi Alexander Safran, of Bucharest, Rumania, made the following statement on April 7, 1944, to papal nuncio Andrea Cassulo: "In the most difficult hours which we Jews of Rumania have passed through, the generous assistance of the Holy See...was decisive and salutary. It is not easy for us to find the right words to express the warmth and consolation we experienced because of the concern of the supreme pontiff, who offered a large sum to relieve the sufferings of deported Jews.... The Jews of Rumania will never forget these facts of historic importance."

Chief Rabbi Isaac Herzog

Jewish organizations took note of Pius XII's efforts, and they turned to him in times of need. Chief Rabbi Isaac

Herzog wrote to Cardinal Maglione on behalf of Egyptian Jews expressing thanks for the Holy See's charitable work in Europe and asking for assistance for Jews being held prisoner in Italy. The following month he wrote back thanking Pius for his efforts on behalf of the refugees that "had awakened a feeling of gratitude in the hearts of millions of people."

As noted earlier, on August 2, 1943, the Jewish Congress sent the following message to Pope Pius XII suggesting that he ask the Italian authorities "to remove as speedily as possible to southern Italy or other safer areas twenty thousand Jewish refugees and Italian nationals now concentrated in internment camps... and so prevent their deportation and similar tragic fate which has befallen Jews in Eastern Europe."

In September, a representative from the World Jewish Congress reported to the Pope that approximately four thousand Jews and Yugoslav nationals who had been in interment camps were removed to an area that was under the control of Yugoslav partisans. As such, they were out of immediate danger. The report went on to say: "I feel sure that the efforts of your Grace and the Holy See have brought about this fortunate result, and I should like to express to the Holy See and yourself the warmest thanks of the World Jewish Congress. The Jews concerned will probably not yet know by what agency their removal from danger has been secured, but when they do they will be indeed grateful."

A few months later, Rabbi Herzog again wrote to Pope Pius XII expressing his "sincere gratitude and deep appreciation for so kind an attitude toward Israel and for such valuable assistance given by the Catholic Church to the endangered Jewish people." Jewish communities in Chile, Uruguay, and Bolivia also sent similar offers of thanks to the Pope.

10

Conclusion

Should Yad Vashem Honor Pius XII?

In 1982, the Pope's private secretary and housekeeper, Sister Pascalina Lehnert, wrote her memoirs: *Ich durfte ihm dienen: Erinnerungen an Papst Pius XII.* In them she explicitly states that Eugenio Pacelli warned the Germans against Adolf Hitler in 1929, four years before the dictator came into power on January 30, 1933. When asked if Hitler could perhaps help the German people, Pacelli shook his head and said: "Who among you has at least read his horrifying book *Mein Kampf?* I would be very much mistaken in thinking that all this could end well." The future Pope Pius XII could not understand why even highly competent Germans did not share his totally negative judgment.

No one can deny the historical record which shows that Pope Pius XII, through his network of apostolic delegates throughout the world, was able to save the lives of thousands of Jews during the Holocaust. As early as April 4, 1933, Cardinal Eugenio Pacelli ordered the apostolic nuncio in Berlin "to intervene with the government of the Reich on behalf of the Jews and point out all the dangers involved in an anti-Semitic policy." The Catholic Church, therefore, did not simply protest on behalf of Church interests during negotiations of the concordat, but protested on behalf of persecuted Jews when the new Hitler regime announced a major boycott of Jewish businesses. The record shows that more than sixty protests were made by Pope Pius XII. Across the theater of war, prisoners and refugees appealed to Pius XII as the representative of an older and more exacting morality than that practiced in the so-called "New Europe."

Leaders throughout the world were deaf to Pius XII's words before World War II: "Nothing is lost by peace. Everything may be lost by war." His was the outstanding religious voice that openly and consistently defied the Nazis. While some individuals betrayed their Jewish friends by revealing their destinations, the Pope's so-called "silence" saved lives. Had he spoken out, would not many more lives have been destroyed? It is foolish to think that the assistance given Jews, in the Vatican and in Rome alone, would have been successful without his knowledge and protection. Pope Pius XII provided food and other necessities to the thousands of victims hidden in convents and monasteries during the Nazi occupation of Rome.

The work of the Vatican Information Office is described in my *Crusade of Charity: Pius XII and POWs.* This book shows how Pius XII consoled and inspired people in all walks of life, of all ages and religious convictions. Expressed in letters addressed directly to Pius XII, Jews and non-Jews confided their dreams, sorrows, and hopes. Young and old appealed to Pius XII for help in locating missing loved ones. The only link for prisoners of war to a voice of friendship was that of Pius XII through the Vatican Information Office. Their hope was based on the interest expressed by the Pope who inspired and comforted them with the visits of his representatives. It explains what Pius XII did to help save Jews, what he did to help the prisoners of war during World War II. Vatican documents describe Pope Pius XII's efforts to terminate the war and to mitigate its tragic effects.

The Vatican Information Office offered a powerful system for prisoners of war to communicate with their loved ones. Young and old, Jews and Christians appealed to Pius XII for help in locating missing sons, husbands, relatives, and friends. This office dealt with the 20 million requests and provided information to comfort the distraught. It is the fascinating story of the grieved and heroic people in their own words interspersed with letters, telegrams, and reports of the apostolic delegates who, at the direction of the Pope, visited prisoners in camps spread around the world. Clearly it is time to stop the misrepresentations with regard to the role played by the Catholic Church during World War II.

Critics who judge Pius XII's honesty and loyalty must consider that he lived profoundly the spiritual drama of the victims. He served the cause of religion by defending the rights of humanity. He invoked peace and freedom for all. He was an indefatigable pastor, a teacher of justice, honor, and loyalty. Not only did he provide money, ships, and food, but he placed his radio, his diplomacy, his convents, at the disposal of the refugees. What would survivors have preferred — words or actions? If he had publicly condemned Hitler or Mussolini, would thousands of Jews have survived who otherwise would have been killed? Would the Nazis and the Fascists have tolerated the charitable work of the Catholic Church during World War II?

When some five hundred Jews embarked at Bratislava on a steamer for Palestine, their ship tried to enter the seaport of Istanbul but was refused permission. Captured by an Italian patrol boat, the Jews were imprisoned in a camp at Rhodes. One of the prisoners managed to appeal to Pius XII for help. Thanks to the Pope's intervention, unknown to the Axis, the refugees were transferred to an improvised camp (Ferramonti-Tarsia) in southern Italy, where they were found safe three years later, in December 1943.

The Nazis had solidified their power in the early 1930s, and ferocious retaliation had been the typical response to every Vatican protest. Tibor Baransky, a board member of the U.S. Holocaust Memorial Council and a Yad Vashem honoree, recalls that "papal nuncios helped the Jews. They got their orders straight from the Pope." He recounted that, while working at the age of twenty-two as a special representative of Angelo Rotta, the papal nuncio in Hungary, he heard from Jewish leaders who asked the Pope not to raise a public outcry over the Nazi atrocities — since it would likely only increase their ferocity. Working with Rotta, Baransky carried documents, forged protective passes, and faked baptismal certificates to save as many Jewish lives as possible.

When news of Pius XII's death on October 9, 1958, was flashed around the world, an editorial, "Fighter for Peace," in the *Los Angeles Examiner* expressed the sentiments of Catholics and non-Catholics, and declared that this *Fighter for Peace* was the *Pope of Peace*. Of those mourning the Pope's death, Jews — who credited him with being one of their greatest benefactors — were in the forefront.

Elio Toaff, chief rabbi of Rome: "More than anyone else, we have had the opportunity to appreciate the great kindness, filled with compassion and magnanimity that the Pope displayed during the terrible years of persecution and terror."

Rabbi Joachim Prinz, national president of the American Jewish Congress: "Among his many great contributions to mankind, the Pontiff will be remembered wherever men of good will gather for his profound devotion to the cause of peace and for his earnest efforts in the rescue of thousands of victims of Nazi persecution, including many Jewish men, women and children."

Bernard Baruch: "During a dark generation of war, hate, and unspeakable crimes against humanity, he helped keep burning the torch of peace, love, and brotherhood. He epitomized the nobility of which the human soul is capable. To men of all faiths he was an inspiration and an example of courage, dedication, and selflessness.

"The Talmud teaches us 'whoever saves a life receives as much credit as if he had saved an entire world.' If this is true — and it is just as true as the most typical of all Jewish principles: that of the holiness of human life — then a Jew must also defend loudly a great saver of Jewish life."

Far more than two million Jews did indeed survive, thanks to the help of the Church, bishops, priests, and laymen. Undoubtedly, Pius XII deserves "that forest in the Judean hills which kindly people in Israel proposed for him in October 1958. A memorial forest, like those planted for Winston Churchill, King Peter of Yugoslavia, and Count Bernadotte of Sweden with 860,000 trees."

The media has both praised and criticized the actions of Pope Pius XII and the Catholic Church in trying to save Jews hunted down by the Nazis. With so much available documentation, it is incredible that the debate over the actions of Pope Pius XII has not terminated.

Pope Pius XII refused to publicize his own good deeds. A story in the *International Herald Tribune* (October 22, 2001) is part of the official war record in Italy. From

1943 to 1945, Leonardo Marinelli was a commander in the Royal Finance Guard in the Aprica internment camp, located in northern Italy. His *Diary* records an entry for September 12, 1943. It is one of the many examples of Pius XII's actions on behalf of Jewish refugees. According to this *Diary* the Pope sent Giuseppe Carozzi, a young Italian priest, to Marinelli requesting that three hundred Jewish Yugoslav internees be given permits to Switzerland. Despite strict Nazi orders forbidding Jews, prisoners of war, or anyone who had not joined Mussolini's northern Italian puppet Republic of Salò from crossing the border, Marinelli complied with the Pope's wishes. As the group crossed the border during the next four days, guards were seen "carrying bags for some of the fugitives."

Marinelli himself was placed in an internment camp by the Nazis. He escaped. In his testimony to the Finance Guard high command in July 1945, Marinelli confirmed what he had written in his *Diary*.

As a result of Pius XII's directives, many Jews survived and have left testimonials, interviews, and public acknowledgments toward the Pope, the Catholic Church, and its religious organizations. Those who doubt that Jews were saved also offend the Jews who have testified that they were "saved" by the Vatican during World War II.

But the real object of the controversy is not Pius XII. It is the Chair of Peter. Destroying Pius XII's reputation is only a means to an end: destroying the papacy and the Church as we know it. By denigrating Pius XII, depicted as authoritarian, traditional, and Roman, by painting John Paul II and Benedict XVI with the same brush, some writers are contributing to the goal of many confused Catholics — changing the Church into a social institution.

In his 1963 monograph, Dr. Joseph Lichten, head of the Intercultural Affairs Department of the Anti-Defamation League of B'nai B'rith, questioned: "What is the case against Pius XII? In brief, that as head of one of the most powerful moral forces on earth he committed an unspeakable sin of omission by not issuing a formal statement condemning the Nazis' genocidal slaughter of the Jews, and that this silence was motivated by reasons considered in modern times as base: political exigency, economic interests, and personal ambition.

"What is the case for him? That Pope Pius XII did everything humanly possible to save lives and alleviate suffering among the Jews; that a formal statement would have provoked the Nazis to brutal retaliation, and would substantially have thwarted further Catholic action on behalf of Jews."

The Second Vatican Council's Declaration on the Relationship of the Church to Non-Christian Religions (*Nostra Aetate*) explains that the Jewish roots of Christianity oblige us to overcome the conflicts of the past and to create new bonds of friendship and collaboration. It affirms in particular that the Church deplores all forms of hatred or persecution directed against the Jews and all displays of anti-Semitism at any time and from any source.

On January 17, 2007, Pope Benedict XVI stated: "To grow and be fruitful, the Judeo-Christian friendship must also be based on prayer . . . a persistent prayer to the Lord that Jews and Christians may respect and appreciate one another and collaborate together for justice and peace in the world."

Indeed, it is time for Yad Vashem to acknowledge the truth, and to bestow the title "Righteous Among the Nations" upon His Holiness Pope Pius XII, one of the greatest benefactors of Jews in modern times.

Chronology

Pius XII's Life (1876–1958)

The following chronology is a partial listing of important dates in the life of Pope Pius XII and includes statements showing that he was not anti-Semitic. As secretary of state, Cardinal Eugenio Pacelli condemned strongly the anti-Semitic persecutions in Germany. On March 2, 1939, Cardinal Pacelli became Pope Pius XII. He urged the Christian restoration of family life and education, the reconstruction of society, the equality of nations, the suppression of hate propaganda, and the formation of an international organization for disarmament and the maintenance of peace. He openly condemned the oppression of invaded lands and the inhuman conduct of World War II.

As successor of St. Peter, Pope Pius XII walked in the shoes of the Fisherman in troubling times with a faith that did not fail. He was a highly respected twentieth-century Church leader who spoke out on many issues of moral concern and public policy: these statements laid the foundations for the Second Vatican Council's document, *Gaudium et Spes,* on the Church in Today's World.

◆ ◆ ◆

1876 *March 2*. Born in Rome, Italy, of Virginia Graziosi and Filippo Pacelli. Two days later, in the Church of Saints Celso and Giuliano, baptized Eugenio Maria Giuseppe Giovanni.

1880 Eugenio Pacelli entered kindergarten and then attended elementary school.

1886 Received First Holy Communion.

1891 Studied at the Ennio Quirino Visconti Lyceum.

1894 Entered the Capranica Seminary in October; enrolled at Gregorian University.

1895 Suffered a physical setback, requiring him to live at home while continuing his studies. Registered in the Sapienza School of Philosophy and Letters and at the Papal Athenaeum of St. Apollinaris for Theology. Received the baccalaureate and licentiate degrees *summa cum laude*.

1899 *April 2.* Ordained a priest. Assigned as curate to the Chiesa Nuova. Continued studies for a doctorate in canon law and civil law at the Apollinaris.

1901 Served as a research aide in the Office of the Congregation of Extraordinary Ecclesiastical Affairs. When Queen Victoria died, Pope Leo XIII sent Father Pacelli to London with a personal handwritten letter of condolence for her son, King Edward II.

1904 Named a papal chamberlain with the title of Monsignor; became a domestic prelate the following year.

1908 Attended the Eucharistic Congress in London and two years later represented the Holy See at the Coronation of King George V.

1911 *March 7.* Appointed assistant secretary of the Congregation of Extraordinary Ecclesiastical Affairs.

1912 *June 20.* Became pro-secretary of the Congregation of Extraordinary Ecclesiastical Affairs.

1914 *February 1.* Became secretary of the Congregation.

1916   *February 9.* In response to an appeal by the American Jewish Committee on December 30, 1915, that Pope Benedict XV use his moral influence to speak out against anti-Semitism, Pacelli became deeply involved in the preparation of a pro-Jewish document signed by Vatican secretary of state Cardinal Gasparri. His statement appeared in the *New York Times,* April 17, 1916, under the headline: "Papal Bull Urges Equality for Jews."

1917   *April 20.* Appointed nuncio to Bavaria, Germany.

       May 13. Consecrated bishop and elevated to the rank of archbishop.

       May 28. Presented his credentials to Ludwig III, king of Bavaria.

1920   *June 22.* Appointed first apostolic nuncio of Germany.

1924   *March 29.* Signed a concordat with Bavaria, which was ratified by the Bavarian Parliament, January 15, 1925. Left Munich for residence in Berlin.

       June 14. Concluded a concordat with Prussia, ratified two months later by the Prussian Parliament.

       December 16. Recalled to Rome, where he received a cardinal's hat.

1930   *February 7.* Appointed secretary of state. On March 25, 1930, became archpriest of the Vatican Basilica.

1932   Reviewed Nuncio Cesare Orsenigo's New Year's discourse and by secret code told him to eliminate a paragraph that praised Hitler and to remove the words "Leader of the German people."

1933   *April 4.* Ten days after the "Enabling Act," as the apostolic nuncio in Berlin was ordered "to intervene with the government of the Reich on behalf of the Jews and point out all the dangers involved in an anti-Semitic policy."

   July 20. Signed the concordat with Germany in order to protect the German Catholics and the Church. Hitler signed this agreement, promising freedom of religion; five days later Hitler abolished the Catholic Youth Movement and forbade the publication of Catholic newspapers and religious processions.

1934   *October 10–14.* Presided as papal legate at the International Eucharistic Congress in Buenos Aires, Argentina.

1935   *March 12.* In an open letter to Cardinal Schulte of Cologne, attacked the Nazis as "false prophets with the pride of Lucifer."

   April 25–28. Spoke at Lourdes, as Pope Pius XI's delegate to France, for the closing days of the jubilee year honoring the nineteenth centenary of Redemption. Delivered an address before a quarter of a million people. Described the Nazis as "possessed by the superstition of race and blood" and declared that "the Church does not consent to form a compact with them at any price." The *New York Times* headlined its story: "Nazis Warned at Lourdes" (April 29, 1935).

1936   *October 8.* Arrived in the United States of America on the *Conte di Savoia,* for an "unofficial" trip covering some eight thousand miles chiefly by plane, as he made an in-depth study of the American Church.

1937   Traveled to France in July as cardinal-legate to conse-
       crate and dedicate the new basilica in Lisieux during the
       Eucharistic Congress.

1938   *April 19*. Assured Joseph P. Kennedy, U.S. ambassador
       to Great Britain, that any political compromise with the
       Nazis was "out of the question."

1939   *March 2*. Becomes the 262nd Pope. Takes the name of
       Pius XII and speaks in his first address to the cardinals
       about true and lasting peace. His motto indicated peace
       to be a fruit of justice: *Opus justitiae pax* (Isa. 34:17).

       March 12. Issued a call for a peace conference of Euro-
       pean leaders involving Italy, France, England, Germany,
       and Poland.

       August 24. Last-minute appeal to head off the outbreak
       of World War II: "I appeal again to governments and
       their peoples.... Nothing is lost by peace. Everything
       may be lost by war.... Let men start to negotiate again."

       September 1. World War II began as the Nazis invaded
       Poland. Pius XII urged that "in occupied territory the
       lives, the property, the honor, the religious convictions
       of the inhabitants will be respected."

       October 20. Issued his first encyclical, *Summi Pontifica-
       tus* (On the Unity of Human Society), which attacked
       totalitarianism and racism. Restated that there could be
       no difference made between Jews and non-Jews. The
       Nazis were clearly condemned in this encyclical. The
       head of the Gestapo, Heinrich Müller, wrote: "This
       encyclical is directed exclusively against Germany, both
       in ideology and in regard to the German-Polish dispute.

How dangerous it is for our foreign relations as well as our domestic affairs is beyond question."

December 25. In his Christmas message to the cardinals, outlined a five-point plan — the requisites for a just and honorable peace.

1940 *January 21.* Vatican Radio Station broadcast in many languages a description and denunciation of German policy in Poland.

January 27. Vatican Radio and *L'Osservatore Romano* revealed to the world the dreadful cruelties of tyranny that the Nazis were inflicting on the Jewish and Catholic Poles.

Easter. Pius XII condemned the invasions of Belgium, Holland, and Luxemburg and referred to a world poisoned by lies and disloyalty and wounded by excesses of violence.

May 10. After the invasion by the Germans, sent telegrams to comfort the sovereigns of Belgium, Holland, and Luxemburg.

December 6. Ordered the Congregation of the Holy Office to issue a formal and explicit condemnation of the mass murder going on in Germany in the name of improving the race.

1941 *Easter.* Pius XII's radio message: "Let us pray for universal peace; not for peace based upon the oppression and destruction of peoples but peace which, while guaranteeing the honor of all nations, will satisfy their vital needs and insure the legitimate rights of all ... peace that will be just, in accordance with human and Christian norms."

December 25. The *New York Times* described Pius XII's Christmas message: "The voice of Pius XII is a lonely voice in the silence and darkness enveloping Europe this Christmas.... In calling for a 'real new order' ... the Pope put himself squarely against Hitlerism."

1942 *December 25.* Another editorial of the *New York Times* praised the Pope: "This Christmas more than ever he is a lonely voice crying out of the silence of a continent."

1943 *April 30.* Letter to Bishop (later Cardinal) von Preysing of Berlin states: "In spite of good reasons for Our open intervention, there are others equally good for avoiding greater evils by not interfering. Our experience in 1942, when We allowed the free publication of certain Pontifical documents addressed to the Faithful, justifies this attitude."

June 2. Addressed the dilemma of the extermination of the Jews in a communication to the Sacred College of Cardinals. He called attention to "the anxious entreaties of all those who because of their nationality or their race are being subjected to overwhelming trials and, sometimes, through no fault of their own, are doomed to extermination.... Every word We address to the competent authority on this subject, and all Our public utterances, have to be carefully weighed and measured by Us in the interests of the victims themselves, lest, contrary to Our intentions, We make their situation worse and harder to bear."

June 29. Issued *Mystici Corporis Christi,* which attacked National Socialism.

July 19. When American bombers dropped hundreds of tons of explosives on Rome, Pius XII hurried from the Vatican to comfort the injured, administer the Last Rites, and distribute money to those in need of food and clothing. The Romans gave him the title *Defensor Civitatis.*

September. When the Germans took control in Italy, Pius XII lifted the obligation of "enclosure" in convents and monasteries and instructed the religious to open their doors to Jews, refugees, and other victims of oppression, thus saving many thousands of Jews from deportation and death. In the Vatican itself and in Castelgandolfo, the papal summer residence, thousands were sheltered and provided for by the Pope himself.

September 30. The encyclical on biblical studies, *Divino Afflante Spiritu,* encouraged students of the written word of God to use fully the fruits of modern research.

1944 *March 9.* A telegram (No. 2341) reprinted in *From Hitler's Doorstep: The Wartime Intelligence Reports of Allen Dulles, 1942–45,* confirms that "Jews and other refugees were hidden in the pontifical palace in Castelgandolfo when the Allies bombed the village. The Vatican protested the bombing of its territory."

July 14. The American Hebrew in New York published an interview with Rome's chief rabbi Israel Zolli, who had been hidden in the Vatican during the German occupation of Rome. He stated: "The Vatican has always helped the Jews and the Jews are very grateful for the charitable work of the Vatican, all done without distinction of race."

December 1. The *New York Times* reported that the World Jewish Congress publicly thanked the Holy See for its protection of Jews, especially in Hungary. The following year (October 1945), the World Jewish Congress made a financial gift to the Vatican in recognition of the Vatican's work to save the Jews.

1946 *January 6.* In a letter to Catholic bishops, Pius XII spoke about the sufferings of abandoned children and the dangers they were exposed to as very close to his heart.

1947 *March 21.* On the fourteenth centenary of St. Benedict, Pius XII issued *Fulgens Radiatur,* which expressed the need for the restoration of the Abbey of Montecassino, destroyed in World War II, to serve as a symbol of faith in an unstable world.

September 11. Papal Directives for the Woman of Today, Pius XII's address to the Congress of the International Union of Catholic Women's Leagues, Rome, Italy, states: "Women must safeguard the rights of the family and participate in the social and political life of the world."

1949 *Christmas.* In his Christmas message for the 1950 Holy Year (Jubilee Year of the Redemption) Pius XII appealed to all Catholics to besiege heaven with continuous prayers ... for world peace ... and for social justice and charity for those in want.

1952 *May.* In a speech to nurses, Pius XII asked the question: "What should we have done that we have not done?"

July 7. Wrote an apostolic letter to the people of Russia, with the prayer "that they enjoy, together with a just and reasonable material prosperity, that freedom also through which every one of you may be able to safeguard your human dignity, to know the teachings of the true religion and to give due worship to God, not only in the inner sanctuary of your own conscience but also openly, in public and private life."

1953   *August 27.* Signed a concordat with Spain.

1954   *April.* Addressed a group of English doctors: "The doctor has been appointed by God Himself (cf. Eccl. 38:1) to minister to the needs of suffering humanity. He who created that fever-consumed or mangled frame, now in your hands, who loves it with an eternal love, confides to you the ennobling charge of restoring it to health."

1955   *May 26.* As a gesture of thanks to Pope Pius XII for his services to Jews during the war, the Israeli Philharmonic gave a command performance of Beethoven's Seventh Symphony at the Vatican.

1956   *October 14.* Addressed the Federation of Italian Women: "In virtue of a common destiny here on earth . . . there is no field of human activity that must remain closed to women. Her horizons reach out to the regions of politics, work, the arts, sports — but always in subordination to the primary functions fixed by nature itself."

Holy Week liturgy reformed, removing the reference to Jews.

1957   *December 24.* Pope Pius XII's Christmas message ended with these words: "*Peace* is a 'good' so precious, so desirable, and so desired that every effort to defend it, even at the cost of sacrificing one's own aspirations, is a 'good' well spent." His last public word was "Peace."

1958   *October 5.* Ended his last discourse to the members of the Latin Notary Congress exhorting his audience to do its duty with regard to the "conservation of *Peace,* which is desired by all men of good will."

October 9. Death of Pope Pius XII.

◆ ◆ ◆

The documents and history confirm that Pius XII was indeed a champion of peace, freedom, and human dignity, a pastor who encouraged Catholics to look on Christians and Jews as their brothers and sisters in Christ, all children of a common Father. Pius XII was aware of the danger that Communism would spread in Western Europe. He suffered with those who were persecuted by the Communists and called for a special Consistory of cardinals to discuss the persecution of the Church in Eastern Europe. Through his personal efforts, the Communists were defeated in the 1948 Italian elections.

Bibliography

Actes et documents du Saint Siège relatifs à la Seconde Guerre Mondiale. Vatican City: Libreria Editrice Vaticana, 1965–81, Tomes I–XI (Tome III in 2 vols.), edited by Pierre Blet, Robert A. Graham, Angelo Martini, and Burkhart Schneider.

Archives of the Congregation for Extraordinary Ecclesiastical Affairs (Secretariat of State).

Blet, Pierre, S.J. *Pius XII and the Second World War: According to the Archives of the Vatican.* Paris: Perrin, 1997, translated by Lawrence J. Johnson. New York and Mahwah, N.J.: Paulist Press, 1999.

Bottum, Joseph, and David G. Dalin, *The Pius War: Response to the Critics of Pius XII.* With an Annotated Bibliography of Works on Pius XII, the Second World War, and the Holocaust by William Doino Jr. Lanham, Md., and New York: Lexington Books, 2004.

Breitman, Richard. *Official Secrets: What the Nazis Planned, What the British and Americans Knew.* New York: Hill and Wang, 1998.

Dalin, David G. *The Myth of Hitler's Pope: How Pope Pius XII Rescued Jews from the Nazis.* Washington, D.C.: Regnery Publishing, 2005.

Dulles, Allen Welsh. *From Hitler's Doorstep: The Wartime Intelligence Reports of Allen Dulles, 1942–45.* Ed. Neal H. Petersen. University Park: Pennsylvania State University Press, 1996.

Frankl, Viktor E., and Pinchas Lapide. *Ricerca di Dio e domanda di senso: Dialogo tra un teologo e uno psicologo* (A quest for God and the meaning of life). Torino: Edizioni Claudiana, 2006.

Gallo, Patrick J., ed. *Pius XII, the Holocaust and the Revisionists.* Jefferson, N.C.: McFarland & Company, 2006.

Gilbert, Martin. *The Holocaust: A History of the Jews of Europe during the Second World War.* New York: Holt, Rinehart, & Winston, 1985.

———. *Never Again: The History of the Holocaust.* New York: Universe, 2000.

———. *The Righteous: The Unsung Heroes of the Holocaust.* New York: Henry Holt & Company, 2003.

Graham, Robert A. "Pius XII and the Nazis: An Analysis of the Latest Charges That the Pope Was a 'Friend' of the Axis." *America,* December 5, 1964, pp. 742–43.

Hassell, Ulrich von. *The von Hassell Diaries, 1938–1944: The Story of the Forces against Hitler Inside Germany, as Recorded by Ambassador Ulrich von Hassell, a Leader of the Movement.* New York: Doubleday, 1947; reprinted San Francisco: Westview Press, 1994.

Kurzman, Dan. *A Special Mission: Hitler's Secret Plot to Seize the Vatican and Kidnap Pope Pius XII.* Boston: DaCapo Press, 2007.

Levai, Jenö. *Hungarian Jewry and the Papacy: Pius XII Was Not Silent.* London: Sands and Company, 1968.

Marchione, Margherita. *Yours Is a Precious Witness: Memoirs of Jews and Catholics in Wartime Italy.* New York and Mahwah, N.J.: Paulist Press, 1997.

———. *Pius XII: Architect for Peace.* New York and Mahwah, N.J.: Paulist Press, 1999.

———. *Consensus and Controversy: Defending Pius XII.* New York and Mahwah, N.J.: Paulist Press, 2002.

———. *Shepherd of Souls: A Pictorial Life of Pope Pius XII.* New York and Mahwah, N.J.: Paulist Press, 2002.

———. *Crusade of Charity: Pius XII and POWs.* New York and Mahwah, N.J.: Paulist Press, 2006.

Pacepa, Ion Mihai. *Red Horizons: Chronicles of a Communist Spy Chief.* Washington, D.C.: Regnery, 1987.

Poliakov, Léon. *Harvest of Hate: The Nazi Program for the Destruction of the Jews of Europe.* Syracuse, N.Y.: Syracuse University Press, 1954.

Rychlak, Ronald J. *Hitler, the War, and the Pope.* Columbus, Miss.: Genesis Press, and Huntington, Ind.: Our Sunday Visitor Press, 2000.

———. *Righteous Gentiles: How Pius XII and the Catholic Church Saved Half a Million Jews from the Nazis.* Dallas: Spence Publishing Company, 2005.

Tittmann, Harold, Jr. *Inside the Vatican of Pius XII: The Memoir of an American Diplomat during World War II.* New York: Doubleday, 2004.

Toland, John. *Adolf Hitler.* New York: Doubleday, 1976.

Zolli, Eugenio. *Antisemitismo.* Rome: Casa Editrice AVE, 1945.

———. *Before the Dawn.* New York: Sheed and Ward, 1954.

Ten Commandments for Peace

1. Peace is always in God;
   God is Peace.

2. Only men who bow their heads before God are capable of giving the world a true, just, and lasting peace.

3. Unite, all honest people, to bring closer the victory of human brotherhood and with it the recovery of the world.

4. Banish lies and rancor and in their stead let truth and charity reign supreme.

5. Affirm human dignity and the orderliness of liberty in living.

6. Give generously of aid and relief — state to state, people to people, above and beyond all national boundaries.

7. Assure the right of life and independence to all nations, large and small, powerful and weak.

8. Work together toward a profound reintegration of that supreme justice which reposes in the dominion of God and is preserved from every human caprice.

9. The Church established by God as the rock of human brotherhood and peace can never come to terms with the idol-worshippers of brutal violence.

10. Be prepared to make sacrifices to achieve peace.

Pius pp.XII

Index